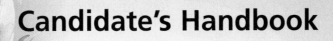

Candidate's Handbook

The Advocate, the Holy Spirit, whom the Father will send in my name, will teach you everything, and remind you of all that I have said to you.

—John 14:26

_____

Candidate's Name

The Ad Hoc Committee to Oversee the Use of the Catechism, United States Conference of Catholic Bishops, has found this catechetical text, copyright 2006, to be in conformity with the *Catechism of the Catholic Church.*

Nihil Obstat: Rev. William M. Becker, STD
                    Censor Librorum
                    August 24, 2005

Imprimatur: †Most Rev. Bernard J. Harrington, DD
                    Bishop of Winona
                    August 24, 2005

The nihil obstat and imprimatur are official declarations that a book or pamphlet is free of doctrinal or moral error. No implication is contained therein that those who have granted the nihil obstat or imprimatur agree with the contents, opinions, or statements expressed, nor do they assume any legal responsibility associated with publication.

The publishing team included Brian Singer-Towns, Lorraine Kilmartin, and John Vitek, development editors; Mary Koehler, permissions editor; prepress and manufacturing coordinated by the prepublication and production services departments of Saint Mary's Press.

Printed in Canada

2804

ISBN 978-0-88489-812-2

 Genuine recycled paper with 20% post-consumer waste.

Candidate's Handbook

Confirmed in a Faithful Community

A Senior High Confirmation Process

Third Edition

Thomas Zanzig

Maura Thompson Hagarty

Saint Mary's Press®

Contents

Welcome!

About This Handbook

This book has been created to make your experience of the process of preparation for Confirmation more enjoyable, fruitful, and memorable. Here's what you will find in this handbook:

Summaries and Additional Insights

The core of each chapter is the summary of the content presented during the Confirmation sessions. The summaries will help you track the program's content, recall information as you need it, or catch up on material if you happen to miss a session.

You are encouraged to read and reflect on the material beyond the formal sessions. Take time at home to read, reflect, and pray on what you are learning in preparation for the reception of the sacrament.

A Chance to Think and Share

The handbook includes a number of short writing exercises—some intended to be strictly personal, such as the journal-writing exercises, and others to be worked on with the other candidates in your group. During the sessions your leader will give you instructions on when and how to complete those exercises, but if your leader does not direct you to do all of them, you may want to do them on your own when you get a chance.

An Invitation to Pray

Prayer is a central part of the process of preparation for Confirmation. This handbook includes resources for both personal and group prayer. Your leader will use many of these resources during the group prayer services that are part of most sessions. Again, if your leader skips some sessions, you might want to privately read the prayers from the skipped sessions.

Catholic Quick Facts

Beginning on page 125 of this handbook is a particularly helpful resource—a special section on major Catholic beliefs and practices. Here you'll find summaries of key Church teachings, a collection of traditional and popular Catholic prayers, and definitions of common terms—many probably familiar, some likely new to you. Sometimes your leader will refer directly to this material. More often, though, you'll find this resource helpful when you need a quick answer to a question about Catholic life and practice.

The Catholic Connection

A recurring feature of this handbook is the Catholic Connection. The Catholic faith is remarkably rich, so much so that in this program, we can barely scratch the surface of the many beliefs and practices that distinguish Catholics. We have to make sure we cover "the basics" of Catholicism. The Catholic Connection essays provide additional insights into how Catholics understand and celebrate those basics. Occasionally during the sessions, the leader may refer to these sections and comment on them. More often, though, you will be encouraged to read and reflect on them on your own.

Heart Links

Sprinkled throughout the handbook are brief readings, poems, and short stories that relate to the themes under discussion. They are intended to catch your attention, to provoke thought, or to offer additional insights. Sometimes they're just for fun! If you find yourself stuck for an idea during the times set aside for journal writing, try browsing through the Heart Links for inspiration. To find them, look for the link icon.

Bible Bytes

Some verses or passages from the Bible are so significant and memorable that we want you to take special note of them. That's what the Bible Bytes are for. Whenever you see one, take a minute to read it. Some day when you need them most, you may "hear" these verses echoing from your memory bank.

Catechism Quotes

The *Catechism of the Catholic Church* is a valuable resource for learning about the Catholic faith. Though it is intended primarily as a reference for bishops, priests, and others who are charged with the task of teaching, laypeople have found it inspirational as well. Throughout this handbook we use excerpts from the *Catechism* to shed additional light on a topic and to provoke thought.

Something to Catch Your Eye . . . and Mind

We hope this book becomes important to you and helps make your Confirmation preparation a special experience. Remember, too, that you'll be able to keep the handbook at the end of the Confirmation process. So consider it a record and keepsake of the whole experience, one that we hope will be of lasting value to you.

Period of Invitation

In this process of preparation for Confirmation, it is important to remember that it is Christ who is the sacrament of our salvation, which we experience through the life of the Church. The sacrament of Confirmation is an efficacious sign of God's grace—that is, the sacrament effects change in us and in the world because of God's power, not our own. The sacrament imparts to the baptized person the fullness of the Holy Spirit, and God's grace bears fruit in our life when those who receive it have the proper inner attitude and readiness. The celebration of the sacrament, in the visible rite, signifies and makes present this grace.

Having already been baptized and received first Eucharist, you now begin preparation for Confirmation with the period of invitation. During these sessions you'll get to know your leader and fellow candidates. You will learn about the meaning of faith and the Church. You also will have an opportunity to reflect on God's call to have faith and to continue the mission of Jesus Christ through full and active membership in the Church. At the end of the period of invitation, you will be invited to continue on your lifelong faith journey by participating in additional sessions designed to help you prepare for Confirmation.

Personal Uniqueness: Promise and Pain

When I look at your heavens,
    the work of your fingers,
    the moon and the stars that
    you have established;
what are human beings that
    you are mindful of them,
    mortals that you care for them?
Yet you have made them a little
    lower than God,
    and crowned them with glory
    and honor.
You have given them dominion over
    the works of your hands;
    you have put all things
under their feet.

—Psalm 8:3–6

About six billion people now live on this big blue marble that we know as Earth. Some have estimated that since the beginning of recorded history, the world has felt the footsteps of over one hundred billion people. The numbers alone are staggering, but listen to this: In the entire history of humanity, no two people have ever been exactly alike.

Each person is unique and therefore special and important. That uniqueness is a gift from God the Father, the creator of everything that exists. All people are called to share in God's own life and to respond to him with love. Because of this relationship, every person has profound dignity and value.

But There's a Downside

Though our origin in God gives us genuine value and dignity as persons, we can forget who—and whose—we are. Sometimes we experience a sense of being lost, confused, unsure about the meaning and value of life, or deeply lonely. Some of these personal struggles, we must admit, we bring on ourselves. We might spend too much time wishing we were someone else, regretting what we think we're missing in life, and envying others who seem to have it all. At other times feelings of doubt, anxiety, and loneliness seem to overtake us when we feel confused about what we're supposed to do in a certain situation, unsure of our abilities, or insecure about the meaning of our life.

At still other times, however, the feelings we experience go much deeper. We feel an ache in our heart when we least expect it, or maybe we feel all alone in the middle of a crowd of people. We might be haunted by the thought that life has little meaning or purpose, or that we are insignificant in an immense universe.

That recurring sense of emptiness in life reflects the deepest hunger of the human heart—the hunger for God. All human beings yearn for union with God, the One who loved them into existence, and they ache when separated from him. This sense of separation—from God, from others, even from ourselves—is at times an expression of the reality of sin, which we will discuss in greater depth later in this program (see pages 51–55). But something even more basic is at work here. Over fifteen hundred years ago, Saint Augustine described this experience as well as anyone ever has: "You have made us for yourself, O Lord, and our hearts are restless until they rest in you."

Being Human

Here in a nutshell is what God has revealed to us about the nature of humanity:

> ‣ All people have dignity and value that comes from God. He created the universe out of goodness and love and yearns to be in relationship with all his creatures, but especially with human beings.

> ‣ We've been created with the ability and option to cooperate with God's will for our lives and for the world or to turn away from him in sin. All too often we choose the latter.

> ‣ God the Father sent his only Son to save us from sin and make eternal life possible for us. Jesus Christ, true God and true man, fully reveals his Father and makes a deep, loving relationship with him possible. This is "redemption."

> ‣ Following Jesus's death, Resurrection, and Ascension from the world, the Holy Spirit inspires us and guides us to holiness.

> ‣ We are called by God to live out the Gospel message and continue Jesus's mission in the world by joining with others in the Church. The Church is in fact the Body of Christ present in the world today, a community enlivened by the Holy Spirit and dedicated to the reign of the Father's love over all creation.

> ‣ We are caught up in the very life of the one God, who has revealed himself to us as the Trinity— Father, Son, and Holy Spirit. We live with the hopeful anticipation that after we die, we will be united with God in a complete and perfect way.

All these marvelous truths will be explored in depth during the process of preparation for Confirmation.

The Process of Preparation at a Glance

You may not experience a "restless heart" as you enter the process of preparation for Confirmation. Each candidate brings his or her own life story to the journey of preparation. The process you are about to begin is designed to help you reflect on and come to terms with many of the big questions of life. In the company of your fellow candidates and with the guidance of leaders in your parish community of faith, you will learn the answers that God has revealed to some of the great mysteries of life: Why are we here? Who is Jesus Christ, and what does he reveal about the meaning of life? How do I experience the presence of God in my life? Why does the Church exist, and why is belonging to it so important?

Yet, O Lᴏʀᴅ, you are our Father;
we are the clay, and you are our potter;
we are all the work of your hand.

—Isaiah 64:8

 The desire for God is written in the human heart.

—*Catechism,* no. 27

The chart below summarizes the process of preparation for Confirmation. Your leader will explain the significance of each step in the process. We invite you to enter into the journey toward Confirmation with honesty and openness. Be ready to share your convictions, your questions, your feelings, your longings. You may be surprised by what God has in store for you. Let the adventure begin!

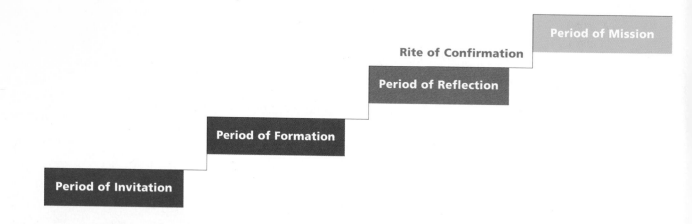

Identity: Looking for the Real You

Who are you? What is your image of yourself? Do you think of yourself as a unique creature of God, endowed with gifts and talents? Is it easier to think of others in this way than it is to think of yourself in this way?

During this session you will have an opportunity to consider these questions and reflect on why you perceive yourself the way you do.

You Are Salt and Light

In his Sermon on the Mount, Jesus said to his disciples: "You are the salt of the earth. . . . You are the light of the world." Read Matthew 5:13–16 in the "Bible Byte" to the right.

When Jesus's listeners imaged the words *salt of the earth,* they would have thought of an oven because salt was used to ignite the fuel used to heat ovens. Wood was not plentiful enough to be used as fuel. Instead, they used something that was readily available: animal dung. They collected it and molded it into patties, which were then salted and left to dry in the sun. On the oven floor, they would place a block of salt, which functioned as a catalyst, enabling the dung patties to catch on fire. After being in use for a while, the salt block would lose its ability to set the fuel afire and would no longer be good for anything except to be "thrown out" onto the road and "trampled under foot."

Jesus's affirming words challenge us to see ourselves as salt, that is, as a catalyst that kindles fires. Of course, we are not talking about literal fires here. Jesus is talking about the fire of his Father's love that binds people together through his Spirit into communities that can transform the world.

When Jesus says, "You are the light of the world," he again affirms his listeners. Light is an image that is used frequently in the Scriptures to symbolize the loving presence of God. Jesus is telling us who we are in terms of God's love. A human being who is light is one who is loved by God and shares that love with everyone. Jesus's incredible affirmation quickly leads to a command: "Let your light shine." Everyone has this God-given potential to be the light of Christ for another person, with the help of the Holy Spirit.

Bible byte

The LORD is gracious and
merciful,
slow to anger and abounding in
steadfast love.
The LORD is good to all,
and his compassion is over all that
he has made.
All your works shall give thanks to
you, O LORD,
and all your faithful shall bless
you.
They shall speak of the glory of your
kingdom,
and tell of your power,
to make known to all people your
mighty deeds,
and the glorious splendor of your
kingdom.
Your kingdom is an everlasting
kingdom,
and your dominion endures
throughout all generations.

—Psalm 145:8–13

Conflicting Messages

Sometimes we hear loud and clear messages that contradict what God has revealed about the value and potential of human beings. These messages come from all over the place: pressure from peers to conform, television shows, movies, advertisements, magazines, the criteria for giving awards to individuals at school and in our communities, and so on. They can drown out God's voice and lead us to view ourselves and others with a mistaken set of values. For example, they can draw us into placing too much value on physical appearance, the things we own, and being number one. Sometimes these messages take the form of stereotypes that keep us from seeing people—even ourselves—the way they really are. When we let these competing messages have power over us, the effect can be likened to keeping salt from sparking fires and putting bushel baskets over lights. The true God-given dignity and giftedness of human beings becomes overshadowed by things that do not have lasting value.

In God's Image

As you search to better understand yourself and to figure out the purpose of your life, try to keep these things in mind: You have been created in the image of God. At your baptism you received the remission of original sin and you also received the grace to begin a new life in Christ. This means, for one thing, that you are full of goodness. In your own unique way, you reflect, like a ray of light, God's goodness and wisdom. God willed you into existence because he loves you. He will never leave you alone. We cannot truly understand who we are apart from God.

Letting Your Light Shine

Read through the following list and check all the things on the list that show how God's light shines through you.

Circle the boxes in front of the three things you are most proud of right now.

Shade in the box before the one item you really want to work on, starting today. Think of one concrete way to improve in that area.

God's light shines through me in . . .

- ❏ my choice of friends who help me make good decisions

- ❏ my love for my family and the way we communicate

- ❏ something I did recently to help another person my own age

- ❏ how I offered friendship to a new person in school

- ❏ the way I try to remain a person of hope

- ❏ something I did recently to help someone older than me

- ❏ a time when I did the right thing even though it was hard

- ❏ my commitment to do my best in school

- ❏ a moment when I offered comfort to someone who was suffering

- ❏ a time when I offered to pray for someone

- ❏ using the gifts God has given me to help others

- ❏ my ability to forgive someone who has hurt me

- ❏ something I had the courage to stand up for

- ❏ sharing with someone who is in need

- ❏ taking time to read the Sacred Scriptures

- ❏ a way in which I helped my family

- ❏ my faith and trust in God

- ❏ my ability to share joy

- ❏ my appearance and how I care for myself

- ❏ a time when I taught something valuable to a child

God provides us with constant evidence of his love through his Son, Jesus Christ.

(Based on Simon, Howe, and Kirschenbaum, *Values Clarification,* pages 136–138)

The light of the world

Reread Matthew 5:13–16. Write about a time when you hid the light of God under a bushel basket. What happened and why? What keeps you from seeing and sharing God's light with others?

Faith: More Than the Eye Can See

The Old Testament tells the story of the Jewish leader Samuel when he was a young boy. One night while in bed, he heard someone calling his name. Thinking it was the priest named Eli, he ran to him and said: "Here I am. You called me." Eli hadn't called Samuel, so he told him to go back to bed. Samuel heard his name and ran to Eli again and again. Finally, when Samuel was awakened for the fourth time by the sound of his name, he recognized God's presence and responded, "Speak, Lord, for your servant is listening" (see 1 Samuel 3:1–10).

Samuel's response to God is an example of faith. God called out to Samuel and revealed his presence. Samuel trusted him and promised to listen. He was ready to hear and to believe God's message.

God calls us, too. In fact, he never stops pursuing us. The Father gave us life because he loves us and wants us to love him and share in his life. Every day of our lives, God communicates his love through the Holy Spirit, who helps us to listen and respond to his message. The gift God gives us to respond to his call—so that we might better know him and live in harmony with his plan for us—is called grace. It is a gift we neither earn nor deserve. We can have faith in God only because of his gift of grace, so faith is also a gift.

However, because God the Father created us with free will, it is up to us to accept his amazing invitation and gift of grace. So faith is also our response to God's grace. It means responding to him with our whole selves—our heart, mind, and will. It means absolute trust in him—letting go and surrendering completely to God's will—and at the same time, faith means believing what God has revealed to us through his deeds and words. However, believing isn't the whole story. Faith includes our acceptance of the "whole truth that God has revealed" (*Catechism*, page 878). When we have faith in God, we recognize that we have our origin in him and that our ultimate goal is to be united with him. Grace inspires us to love him with our whole being. We neither prefer anything to him nor substitute anything in his place. Having faith means that even though God is a mystery beyond words, we realize that he alone is enough—that he is everything we need.

At times, God's creative power and presence are evident to the human eye. But faith allows us to see God's presence even when it isn't obvious.

To See with New Eyes

Faith is a way of hearing, but it is also a way of seeing. The Bible frequently associates faith with words and images related to seeing. Nearly every time the word *seeing* or the notion of seeing appear in the Bible—as, for instance, when blind people are healed or when Jesus accuses someone of "having eyes but not seeing" (see Mark 8:18)—we can be sure the Scriptures are telling us something about the meaning of faith.

Many people live with mental blinders that keep them from truly seeing—seeing the truth of Jesus's message, seeing the meaning of their own life experience, seeing the Holy Spirit at work in the world, even really seeing other people. Their range of vision is often limited by their inability to see new possibilities, to "think outside the box." Or they allow themselves to be blinded by the false promises of our culture—for instance, by the illusion that if they just owned more "stuff" or looked different, they would be happy.

But Jesus calls us to "see with new eyes," to see life the way he sees it. And he shows us how. His teachings and his actions are like a light that helps us see the ultimate meaning and purpose of our lives. He reveals a new understanding of God as Father, Son, and Holy Spirit, and calls us to a life of faith that promises far more than any material possession could ever deliver.

Jesus Christ truly can open our eyes . . . if we let him.

Faith Is a Journey

Even though the knowledge we receive through faith is more certain than any human knowledge can be, we often do not fully understand what God has revealed because of the obstacles mentioned, and because of the nature of what is revealed. Faith is a lifelong journey of coming to know and love God through his Spirit, which makes known to us Christ. It involves searching and asking questions and trying, with the help of the Spirit of God, to rid our lives of the things that keep us from hearing his word and seeing with new eyes. Searching for God demands "every effort of intellect, a sound will, 'an upright heart,'" along with the help of those who can guide us (*Catechism*, number 30).

God's Spirit dwells in the hearts of those who believe in Christ. He will never leave us alone. The Holy Spirit is with us constantly, opening our ears, eyes, and hearts, unveiling Christ to us through the Father's Word.

 We love because [God] first loved us.

—1 John 4:19

Catechism quote Even when he reveals himself, God remains a mystery beyond words: "If you understood him, it would not be God" (Saint Augustine).

—*Catechism,* no. 230

Faith

Choral Reading:
The Healing of the Blind Man

Leader: A reading from the Gospel according to Luke (18:35–43).

Group A: As he approached Jericho, a blind man was sitting by the roadside begging. When he heard a crowd going by, he asked what was happening.

Group B: They told him, "Jesus of Nazareth is passing by." Then he shouted, "Jesus, Son of David, have mercy on me!"

Group A: Those who were in front sternly ordered him to be quiet; but he shouted even more loudly, "Son of David, have mercy on me!"

Group B: Jesus stood still and ordered the man to be brought to him; and when he came near, he asked him, "What do you want me to do for you?"

Group A: He said, "Lord, let me see again."

Group B: Jesus said to him, "Receive your sight; your faith has saved you."

Leader: Immediately he regained his sight and followed him, glorifying God; and all the people, when they saw it, praised God.

Seeing with new eyes

Name one example of blindness that you experience in your attitude toward yourself, in your relationships with others, or in your experience of God. Then express below things that would help you to "see with new eyes" in those areas.

Trusting in God

When we look at the life and Good News of Jesus Christ, we confront the question of what makes for true happiness. The questions Jesus asks are drastically different from those posed by popular culture.

> Popular culture asks, How can I acquire a lot of wealth? Jesus asks, How can I share what I have with those in need?

> Popular culture asks, What do I have to do to be popular? Jesus asks, How can I love all people, even my enemies, without concern for my social status?

> Popular culture asks, How can I gain power over others? Jesus asks, How can I serve others?

The questions Jesus asks lead us to drastically different answers than do the questions posed by our culture. And Jesus's questions lead us to the right answers, to God's revealed truth.

Trust and Faith

All love relationships, all friendships, involve the willingness to trust in the promises of another—promises of fidelity, respect, truthfulness, and so on. The same holds true in our relationship with God. Faith means trusting in God and the truth of his promises—promises made known to us through all he has said and done, but most fully revealed through the life, ministry, death, and Resurrection of Jesus Christ.

The passage in Mark 9:14–29 tells about a father who seeks help from Jesus for his son, who is possessed by a demonic spirit. Jesus tells the father that "all things can be done for the one who believes" (verse 23). The father cries out, "I believe; help my unbelief!" (verse 24). The grace of God is given to us through the Holy Spirit and helps us turn our hearts to God, and it is the Holy Spirit who helps open our minds to understanding and belief. Through the sacraments of Baptism and the Eucharist, we experience the Holy Spirit drawing us to accept and believe the truths of divine Revelation. These truths are not always easy to understand. Sometimes the world we live in seems very different from the world promised to us through faith. What if our willingness to give up our life for others leads only to death—forever and ever? That is where trust and faith come in.

 Who Do You Say That I Am?

Once when Jesus was praying alone, with only the disciples near him, he asked them, "Who do the crowds say that I am?" They answered, "John the Baptist; but others, Elijah; and still others, that one of the ancient prophets has arisen." He said to them, "But who do you say that I am?"

—Luke 9:18–20

 Trust the past to God's mercy, the present to God's love, and the future to God's providence.

—Saint Augustine

Our willingness to place our faith in Jesus Christ is influenced somewhat by what we have to lose. That is why, for example, Jesus talked about the dangers of being rich. Accepting Jesus's teaching about giving rather than taking is easier if we do not have a lot to give in the first place. When it might mean losing something we have worked hard for, it is a lot tougher. Accepting a call to identify with and help poor and oppressed people is difficult when we are comfortable in security and freedom.

The Fullness of Faith

The ultimate outcome for responding to God with faith is to live forever in union with God. Imagine eternity with the one God, whose essence and very being is love! Because of our faith, God forgives all our sins and reconciles us to himself. Without faith this salvation is not possible. "The one who believes and is baptized will be saved; but the one who does not believe will be condemned" (Mark 16:16).

The life of faith is not always easy. We need the support and encouragement of other believers to live the Gospel message even when it is difficult and challenging. That is why faith in Christ means being a baptized and active member of the Catholic Church. Christ promised that the Holy Spirit would guide the Church in a special way, revealing the full truth of the Gospel message. This is what Christ calls us to—with the guarantee that it is worth it, that we will find fullness of faith and give effective witness to the love of God the Father if we do. In the end, with faith, we have nothing to lose and everything to gain!

Who do you say that Jesus is?

In the space below, quickly jot down any names, titles, or descriptive words related to Jesus that immediately come to your mind. Now look back at your list of names or words. In light of those, how would you answer the question that Jesus posed to his disciples: "But who do you say that I am?" (Luke 9:20).

The Church:
A Community of Disciples

No one can believe alone, just as no one can live alone. You have not given yourself faith as you have not given yourself life. The believer has received faith from others and should hand it on to others. Our love for Jesus and for our neighbor impels us to speak to others about our faith. Each believer is thus a link in the great chain of believers. I cannot believe without being carried by the faith of others, and by my faith I help support others in the faith.

—*Catechism,* no. 166

People need people. Life teaches us that we need others not only to survive but to thrive. Research shows a direct link between a person's total health and the number of groups or organizations to which she or he belongs. The God who loved us into existence made us this way; we are hardwired to need one another.

Just as no one can live alone, no one has faith alone. We are able to hear God's call and respond with faith. Our faith is given to us as a gift from God, supported and nourished by the Holy Spirit and by people around us. All the saints who have had faith and gone before us are also an important part of our community. The Church is a people (an assembly) called together (convoked) by God. When God calls us to have faith, he is, at the same time, calling us together to be part of the community of believers called the Church, and the faith we receive is the faith of the Church. Thus the Church—the community of Jesus's disciples—is the mother of all believers.

We must be clear about one thing: The Church is more than simply a human institution, more than a club, more than a social organization. During his earthly ministry, Jesus chose the Apostles and prepared them to continue his mission when he was gone. At the end of his earthly ministry, Jesus promised, "I am with you always, to the end of the age" (Matthew 28:20). This promise was fulfilled at the event called Pentecost, when after Jesus's death and Resurrection, the Holy Spirit came upon the Apostles. By sending the Holy Spirit, Jesus Christ established the community of believers as his own body, the Church, and gave them the responsibility of continuing his mission in the world. This community of faith born by the power of the Holy Spirit is the Body of Christ alive and present in the world today. That is why Pentecost is sometimes referred to as the birthday of the Church.

Take a moment to read the passage from Acts of the Apostles on page 25. That description of the way Christians tried to live immediately after Christ's Resurrection and Ascension paints in broad strokes a portrait of what the Church is called to be. In the Church, the mission of Christ and the Holy Spirit is brought to completion. "Uniting us by faith and Baptism to the Passion and Resurrection of Christ, the Spirit makes us sharers in his life" (*Catechism,* number 2017).

The one and only Church of Christ "subsists" in the Catholic Church. This means that the fullness of the Church is found in the Catholic Church and that only the Catholic Church is fully endowed or gifted with four special qualities called marks of the Church: oneness, holiness, catholicity, and apostolicity.

The Church is one. It is a communion of people called by God and joined to Christ through the indwelling of the Holy Spirit. It acknowledges one Lord, confesses one faith, is born of one baptism, forms only one Body, and is given life by the one Spirit. The Church prays and works with the hope that the unity of all Christians will increase until the end of time, when God's plan will be fulfilled and all divisions will be overcome.

The Church is holy. To be holy is to be united with God. The Church is holy because Christ joined the community of believers to himself as his body. The Church helps its members to conquer sin and grow in holiness so that we are ever more Christlike in our words and our deeds.

The Church is catholic. The word *catholic* means "universal" or "comprehensive." The Church is catholic in two ways. First, the Church's mission is worldwide and extends to the whole human race. Second, God's Revelation through Christ is fully present in the Church; thus the Church offers the fullness of the means of salvation.

The Church is apostolic. An apostle is someone who is sent on a mission. The Church is apostolic in several senses. First, all the members of the Church share in the mission of proclaiming the Good News. Second, the Church's origins are rooted in the faith of the first Apostles. The Church hands on the teaching of the Apostles through the bishops and the Pope, who are the Apostles' successors.

When Catholics pray the Nicene Creed and express belief in "one, holy, catholic, and apostolic Church," we are not claiming to be superior to other Christians, nor are we claiming that as individuals we completely and perfectly embody those qualities. We are aware of our own shortcomings. We pray with the hope that the Church, through the action of the Holy Spirit and the cooperation of its members, will grow in unity and holiness; that the Church will spread the fullness of God's Revelation to all the ends of the earth; and that we will embrace the mission of Jesus Christ as our own.

In all this the Holy Spirit continually guides the Church, constantly reminding us of the powerful message and mission of Jesus Christ and giving us the insight and strength to live according to his message and to embrace his mission.

Where To from Here?

As this session comes to an end, you have an invitation to consider: Is my heart open to exploring more deeply the meaning of the sacrament of Confirmation? You are now invited to consider how the Holy Spirit is moving in your life and the lives of those around you. This is a time to explore the mystery of the sacrament and what it means at a deeper level. It is also a time for you to ask for the grace of an open heart to hear what God is asking of you, as well as a time for a new commitment of understanding.

In the next step of the process of preparation, you will enter into a deeper study of Jesus Christ, his message and his mission. The adventure continues!

All who believed were together and had all things in common; they would sell their possessions and goods and distribute the proceeds to all, as any had need. Day by day, as they spent much time together in the temple, they broke bread at home and ate their food with glad and generous hearts, praising God and having the goodwill of all the people. And day by day the Lord added to their number those who were being saved.

—Acts of the Apostles 2:44–47

Images of the Church

Three New Testament images of the Church reflect a powerful connection between the Church and the Trinity—Father, Son, and Holy Spirit.

The Church as People of God

Long ago God chose the Israelites to be his people and made a covenant with them. Through Jesus Christ, God has made a new covenant in order to fulfill his desire to make all people one body united in love through the Holy Spirit. Those who believe in Christ are the new People of God, "a chosen race, a royal priesthood, a holy nation, God's own people" (1 Peter 2:9). All people are called to enter this one family, the Church, through faith and Baptism.

The Church as Body of Christ

Through the Holy Spirit and the Church's sacraments, Christ establishes the community of believers as his own Body. Saint Paul speaks eloquently about this: "For just as the body is one and has many members, and all the members of the body, though many, are one body, so it is with Christ. . . . Now you are the body of Christ and individually members of it" (1 Corinthians 12:12,27). Comparing the Church with the body highlights the intimate bond between the Church and Christ. All the members, though diverse, are united with one another and with Christ, the head of the body. The Father wants us to become more like his Son and to grow closer to him through the Church.

The union of the members with Jesus is also expressed by the image of a bride and a bridegroom. Christ, the bridegroom, loved the Church, the bride, so much that he formed an everlasting covenant with her. He gave himself up for her and never stops loving her. Because of this the Church is also called the Bride of Christ and is sometimes referred to in the feminine form, that is, as "she."

The Church as Temple of the Holy Spirit

The Church is the dwelling place of the Holy Spirit. Saint Paul asked the people of Corinth, "Do you not know that you are God's temple and that God's Spirit dwells in you?" (1 Corinthians 3:16). Jesus Christ has poured out the Spirit on the members of the Church, making the Holy Spirit part of everything that the Church is and does. The Holy Spirit animates the Body of Christ, the source of its life, its gifts and charisms, and its unity in diversity.

These images emphasize that the Church's essence is unity—unity among all people and with God the Father, Son, and Holy Spirit. The call to have faith and to belong to the Church is an invitation to share in the life and unity of the Trinity, here on earth and after death.

Looking back, looking ahead

Briefly reflect on your experience of the process of preparation to this point. What are your thoughts and feelings as you conclude the period of invitation? Do you hear God's call? Where is it leading you? Is anything holding you back? What questions and concerns would you like to ponder and explore during the next phase of the process, the period of formation?

Personal notes

Period of Formation

We are grateful that you are continuing with the process of preparation for Confirmation. You now enter the period of formation. During these sessions you and your fellow candidates will reflect on Jesus Christ, the Messiah, the savior of the human race. You will explore the Revelation that he is both true God and true man. You may also struggle, as have other believers through the ages, with the causes and the religious meaning of his execution on the cross. And you will delve into the profound meaning of the mysterious event at the heart of Christianity—Jesus's death and Resurrection from the dead. You will also have the opportunity to explore the role of the Holy Spirit in the Church and consider what it means to share in Christ's continuing mission on Earth.

Be prepared to take a deeper, perhaps more mature look at Jesus, one whom you may believe you already know quite well. Try to look at him with the new "eyes of faith" that we discussed during the period of invitation. Some of your past understandings of Jesus may be challenged, while others may be deepened. This we can promise you: You will grow both as a person and as a Christian in the weeks ahead. Why? Because every person who truly encounters Jesus Christ does.

Revelation: Coming to Know Our God

How Do We Learn About Jesus?

We are religious beings by nature and vocation. That is, we come to know God the Father, Jesus Christ, his Son, and the Holy Spirit because God first knows us: "We love because [God] first loved us" (1 John 4:19). From the time we were little children, most of us have learned about Jesus Christ by gathering bits and pieces of information about him over a long period of time. As young children we may hear stories of Jesus from our parents and from other family members. We learn simple prayers addressed to him, sing children's songs about him, or wonder at Christmas images of him in a manger, surrounded by kneeling figures in odd clothing.

Gradually we learn more and more about Christ. We hear Gospel stories about him proclaimed at Mass. We attend religion classes. Slowly we begin to take on the images, understandings, and teachings about Jesus that the Church treasures and preserves. Yet in it all God alone can make known to us the mystery of Christian faith and of Christian life by revealing himself as Father, Son, and Holy Spirit.

But at points in our life—and you may well be experiencing this now—we begin to seek fuller answers to profound questions: What does it mean to have faith in Christ? What does it mean to have the freedom to choose good or evil? How is it that we can choose to believe in God or not believe in him?

When you struggle with questions of faith, struggle with belief in God, or struggle with making moral decisions, you are being exactly what God created you to be—a creature who must make choices. Yet as we have been learning in this preparation, God the Father freely gives us the grace to respond to our vocation of becoming his adopted sons and daughters. It is grace, in the face of our struggles, that draws us into a greater intimacy with the Father, Son, and Holy Spirit through the Church.

God's Revelation

God's Revelation of himself, particularly in the person of Jesus Christ, is his loving invitation to us to be in a trusting relationship. Revelation is God's communication of himself, of his love for us, and of his will that all people would share in his divine life. To the Israelites he revealed that he is the one and only God. Today we affirm God's oneness every time we recite the Nicene Creed and pray, "We believe in one God." To Moses God revealed his name, YHWH, which can be translated "I Am." This mysterious name indicates that God is always present, without origin and without end. Through his words and deeds, he has revealed that his very being is Truth and Love. He will never deceive us and his love for us will never end.

God's Revelation culminates in the person and mission of Jesus Christ. Jesus taught and lived the Good News that God is with us to free us from sin and death. Even more, Jesus himself was revealed as God's Son, both fully God and fully man. As the Christ, he is the messiah, or savior, God promised. Through Christ's life, death, and Resurrection, God makes it possible for us to share eternal life with the Holy Trinity. Through Jesus Christ, God is fully revealed.

We can know all this because God's Revelation is transmitted from generation to generation through the Scriptures and Tradition. The Scriptures are sacred writings that announce God's love and message of salvation. They were written through the inspiration of the Holy Spirit, who guided human authors to write the truth God wished to reveal for the sake of our salvation. Even though it might be hard to see at first, the entire Bible relates to the person, mission, and message of Jesus. The entire biblical record of salvation history points to and finds its fulfillment in Jesus Christ. However, the four Gospels hold a special place for all Christians because they offer the most direct record of Jesus and his teachings.

The word *tradition* is derived from the Latin *traditio,* meaning "transmission" or "handing on." When used in reference to Revelation, Tradition refers to both the process of transmitting God's truth and the truth itself. Tradition includes verbal formulations such as the Nicene Creed and doctrinal teachings. Sometimes this part of Tradition is called the content of the faith. Tradition also includes practices, such as the sacraments, which are essential to the Catholic way of life.

There is a difference between Tradition and traditions. When the Church uses the term tradition with a lowercase *t,* it is referring to customs, expressions, and practices that are not essential to Catholic faith. For example, praying around an Advent wreath and not eating meat on Fridays are traditions. But celebrating Eucharist and believing in God the Father, Son, and Holy Spirit are part of the Tradition. In light of Tradition, which remains unchanged, the Church can adapt or even abandon existing customs and can create new ones.

Both the Scriptures and Tradition communicate the word of God and have their origin in what the Apostles received from Jesus's teaching and example and from the Holy Spirit. They are distinct modes of communication, but closely related. They can never be in conflict, and each one helps us to understand the other.

To ensure that the Scriptures and Tradition would be preserved, Jesus's Apostles left bishops as their successors. Thus the authoritative interpretation of both the Scriptures and Tradition is the task of the Pope, and the bishops acting in communion with him. The Pope and the bishops in their teaching role are also called the Magisterium. With the help of the Holy Spirit, they faithfully teach, interpret, and preserve God's word for every new generation. Jesus's Apostles left bishops as their successors to ensure that this process of transmission would continue without interruption.

Although the Magisterium's teaching role is the authoritative interpretation of the Scriptures and Tradition, it doesn't mean that the rest of us are excused from working to understand and pass on what God has revealed. The *Catechism* reminds us that all the faithful "share in understanding and handing on revealed truth. They have received the anointing of the Holy Spirit, who instructs them[1] and guides them into all truth[2]" (number 91).

The diagram below illustrates how in the Catholic Church, the Scriptures and Tradition work together to hand on knowledge about Jesus Christ to each generation of believers.

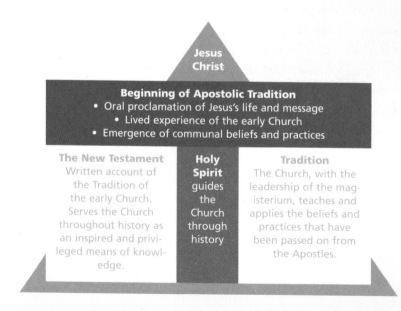

Jesus Christ

Beginning of Apostolic Tradition
- Oral proclamation of Jesus's life and message
- Lived experience of the early Church
- Emergence of communal beliefs and practices

The New Testament
Written account of the Tradition of the early Church. Serves the Church throughout history as an inspired and privileged means of knowledge.

Holy Spirit guides the Church through history

Tradition
The Church, with the leadership of the magisterium, teaches and applies the beliefs and practices that have been passed on from the Apostles.

A Snapshot of Salvation History

Salvation history is the name given to the events, particularly those described in the Bible, that carried forth God's plan to bring us to divine union through his Son, Jesus Christ. Here is a quick overview of that history.

The story of salvation history begins with Creation. As we read in the beginning of the Bible, God created the world and all that is in it, and everything was good. The story of Adam and Eve tells us that God intended us to be in direct communion with him but that the sin of our first parents (original sin) disrupted that perfect communion. Despite that sin, God continued to care for humanity and promised ultimate salvation.

The Bible then describes how the world fell under the domination of sin. Because of their wickedness, God is sorry he made human beings, so he sends a flood to wipe them out. However, God saves a small remnant of good people and makes an everlasting covenant with them. God promises Noah and the whole human race to never destroy the world by flood again. Later he makes another covenant with Abraham, promising that his descendants would be as numerous as the stars and that through him "all the families of the earth shall be blessed" (Genesis 12:3).

Abraham's descendants ended up living for a time in Egypt, where they eventually became slaves. God sent Moses to free the people and lead them to a Promised Land. God entered into yet another covenant with these Israelites, promising that they would be his Chosen People. The Law, with the Ten Commandments as its cornerstone, marked this covenant.

After a period of hardship and wandering, the Israelites eventually entered and settled in the Promised Land. At first they were only a loosely organized association of twelve tribes, but eventually God appointed kings to rule over them. The greatest king was David, who was a brave warrior and charismatic leader. David established Jerusalem as the capital city. After David's death, his son Solomon ruled. Solomon made Jerusalem a mighty city, and he also built an impressive Temple in which to worship God.

Unfortunately, after Solomon's death the kingdom split into two parts, a northern kingdom and a southern kingdom. Two royal lines ruled over those kingdoms for several hundred years. Many of the royalty, the religious leaders, and the people strayed from their covenant with God, falling into idolatry and greed. God raised up prophets to call the people to reform their lives and warn them that if they didn't reform, bad things would happen. And bad things did happen: Assyrians conquered the northern kingdom in

Heart link Most people are bothered by those passages in Scripture which they can't understand; but . . . I have noticed that the passages in Scripture which trouble me the most are those I do understand.

—Mark Twain

721 BC, and the southern kingdom was conquered by the Babylonians in 587 BC. The Babylonians destroyed Jerusalem and the Temple and led the leaders into exile.

At this point the prophets' challenging message became one of hope. They told the people that even though their kingdom had been destroyed, God would not abandon them. They foretold the coming of a savior who would lead the people to peace. After nearly fifty years in exile, a sympathetic Persian king let the people return to rebuild Jerusalem and the Temple. Now known as the Jews, they would never again, until modern times, be an independent nation. Persian, Greek, and Roman governors would rule them until the time of Jesus.

It was into this world that Jesus was born. He was a Jew, a member of the Chosen People, a descendant of King David. He was the Messiah, or anointed one, that the prophets had predicted. Salvation history reaches its climax in Jesus Christ. God has established his new and final covenant with the human race through Christ Jesus's sacrifice: "This cup that is poured out for you is the new covenant in my blood" (Luke 22:20).

After Jesus's Resurrection and Ascension, the Church became visible when the Holy Spirit descended on the Apostles at Pentecost. The Acts of the Apostles and the epistles of the New Testament show us how from the beginning, the Apostles spread the message of God's love by preaching about Jesus Christ and encouraging people to believe in him as Lord and Savior. Through their work the Church grew rapidly, bringing people to Christ to become the worldwide body the Church is today.

Catholic Connection Interpreting the Bible

Not all Christians agree about how reliable information about Jesus Christ is handed on. Revelation is transmitted through both the Scriptures and Tradition, and the value the Church places on these methods is one of the things that make us uniquely Catholic. But some Christians accept only those beliefs and practices clearly identified in the Bible. That is why some of your non-Catholic peers may occasionally challenge some of the Catholic Church's teachings and practices, saying they are nonbiblical.

Differences also occur between Catholics and Fundamentalists, or those Protestants who interpret the Bible literally, regarding the nature of the Scriptures. For example, Catholics (along with many of the larger Protestant denominations) interpret the Gospels in light of the understanding of their

Heart link

When we read the Gospels, we shouldn't listen to Christ speaking to somebody else two thousand years ago, but listen to Him as he speaks to us now.

—Louis Evely

development described on pages 38–39 of this handbook. They contend that we can fully understand the meaning of certain Bible passages only if we take into account when, why, by whom, and to whom they were written. Therefore, Catholics and many Protestants do not expect every word in the Bible to reflect our modern understanding of scientific and historical truth.

Fundamentalist Protestants, on the other hand, accept every word and detail in the Scriptures as factual—including ancient understandings of science and history. This position is called biblical literalism. This difference in the way that Catholics and Fundamentalists understand scientific and historical truth in the Bible accounts for much of the tension between these groups of believers.

Catholic Connection Lectio Divina Shared in Community

Lectio divina is an ancient way of reflecting on and praying the Scriptures. You may be invited to use *lectio divina* as a group during your meeting time. The following steps are one way of using *lectio divina* as a group:

Catholics must both explain and proclaim the Scriptures. To be sure, we must study the Bible, but even more we must live out the truth God reveals to us through it.

1. One person reads aloud the scriptural passage, pausing at the end for one or two minutes of silence. During the silence, group members reflect on a word or phrase that stood out for them.
2. Each person is invited to share aloud the word or phrase that struck him or her. No elaboration is necessary.
3. A different person reads the same passage a second time, pausing for two to three minutes of silence. During the silence, the participants reflect on this question: "How does the word or phrase that has touched my heart touch my life today?"
4. Participants are invited to share their answers aloud, perhaps using the sentence starters "I hear . . ." or "I see . . ."
5. A new person reads the passage a third time, pausing for two or three minutes at the end. During the silence, group members reflect on this question: "What is Christ calling me to do or to become today or this week?"
6. Everyone is invited to share the results of her or his reflection.
7. After everyone who wishes to speak has had the opportunity to do so, everyone prays silently for each person in the group.

Prepare the Way of the Lord: Jesus's Identity Is Revealed

When we look closely and carefully at them, most of the Gospel stories about Jesus are more complex and fascinating than they may first appear. The stories of his baptism and his temptations in the desert offer profound insights into his identity, life, and teachings. In this session we look first at the nature of the Gospels themselves and then at these intriguing stories about Jesus.

The Development of the Gospels

The Gospels tell us, through the eyes of faith, about Jesus's life and mission. Though the Gospels contain biographical and historical material, their authors did not aim to report on events in the way a modern historian or biographer would. Rather, the Gospels are proclamations of faith or faith testimonies that were written years after the death and Resurrection of Jesus. They share the deeds and words of faith in a way that reveals God's truth, and they cannot be separated. This means that the authors, inspired by the Holy Spirit, told the story of Jesus in light of their belief in him as their Messiah and, indeed, as the Son of God. We learn from what Jesus did and also from what Jesus said, for he taught us how to live a life in the truth of God.

The chart on page 41 summarizes how the four Gospels developed during the sixty or so years following Jesus's death and Resurrection. We can identify at least three major stages in the development of the Gospels:

1. *The life and teaching of Jesus.* During the time of Jesus's public ministry, his words and his actions had a profound effect on his disciples.
2. *The oral tradition.* After the death and Resurrection of Jesus, the disciples and the early Church proclaimed the Good News of Jesus throughout the Roman Empire. During this time they recalled, shared, and collected stories and sayings by and about Jesus.

Bible byte

Indeed, the word of God is living and active, sharper than any two-edged sword, piercing until it divides soul from spirit, joints from marrow; it is able to judge the thoughts and intentions of the heart.

—Hebrews 4:12

3. *The written Gospels.* Later, human authors called Evangelists wrote the Gospels, a title based on a word for "good news." The four Evangelists, working more like editors than as authors of original material, compiled sayings and stories that had been handed on through the years. The Evangelists organized the material and offered explanations in an effort to clearly and effectively announce the Good News to the particular audiences they were addressing.

Baptized in the Jordan

Jesus's baptism in the Jordan River by John the Baptist marks the beginning of his public life and signifies his public acceptance of his mission on Earth. In the Gospel stories of the baptism, the voice of God the Father calls out and announces that Jesus is his beloved Son, and the Holy Spirit comes upon Jesus. For our purposes it is important to recognize that the baptism stories express two central insights about Jesus's identity:

> ❯ Jesus is the Son of God the Father.

> ❯ The Father anointed Jesus with the Holy Spirit.

The Father sent his only Son, Jesus Christ, so that we might know his love. Jesus came to save us from sin and death and to reconcile us with God. Jesus, himself God, took on human nature without losing his divine nature. He did this so that we might share in his divinity and have eternal life, which is his mission.

The Church calls the mystery of the union of two natures in one divine person the Incarnation (from the Latin *incarnatio,* meaning "becoming flesh"). The Gospel of John expresses the mystery of Jesus's identity in this way: "And the Word became flesh and lived among us" (John 1:14). The common phrase used in Catholic teaching is that Jesus Christ is both "true God and true man." Because in Jesus Christ the human and the divine are perfectly united, he is the perfect and only mediator between God and humanity. God is able to fully reveal his loving plan for us through Jesus Christ. By believing in him and in giving ourselves to him with our whole heart, mind, and soul, the Holy Spirit will help us become more fully the image of God, which is our ultimate destiny.

 Christ became what we are in order that we might become what he is.

—Saint Athanasius

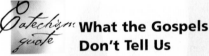 **What the Gospels Don't Tell Us**

Many things about Jesus of interest to human curiosity do not figure in the Gospels. Almost nothing is said about his hidden life at Nazareth, and even a great part of his public life is not recounted.[3] What is written in the Gospels was set down there "so that you may believe that Jesus is the Christ, the Son of God, and that believing you may have life in his name."[4]

—*Catechism,* no. 514

In the beginning
   when God created the heavens
     and the earth,
the earth was a formless void
   and darkness covered the face
     of the deep. . . .
Then God said,
   "Let there be light."

—Genesis 1:1–3

Titles of Jesus

Jesus's names and titles in the New Testament give us insight into his identity and mission:

> **Jesus.** In Hebrew, *Jesus* means "God saves." This signifies who Jesus was—God—and what he came to earth to do—save us.

> **Christ.** This title is the Greek translation of the Hebrew word *messiah,* which means "anointed one." The Gospel accounts of Jesus's baptism reveal that Jesus is the one anointed for mission by God the Father with the power of the Holy Spirit. He is the Messiah, the savior the Jewish people were waiting for.

> **Son of God.** This title, when applied to Jesus, signifies his unique relationship with the Father. He is the only eternal Son of the Father and is God himself.

> **Lord.** The Jews regarded the Hebrew name for God, Yahweh, to be too sacred to say out loud, so they used Lord instead. So when we call Jesus "Lord," we are expressing our belief that he is God.

Jesus Was Tempted . . . and So Are We

Following their accounts of the baptism of Jesus, the Gospels of Matthew, Mark, and Luke tell the story of Jesus's temptation by Satan after forty days in the desert without eating. Behind all the marvelous imagery of that story, a basic message is conveyed: In the face of temptation, Jesus does not sin. The three temptations (to turn stones into bread, to survive a leap from the top of the Temple, and to gain control of the kingdoms of the world) each reflect a different value or source of power, and in each case, Jesus refuses Satan while revealing that the Son of God is the Messiah. Jesus is sometimes called the new Adam because, unlike the original Adam who gave in to temptation, Jesus is one with the Father. Furthermore, just as Adam's sin was passed on to the rest of humanity, Jesus vanquished the Tempter, making it possible for us to unite ourselves with his saving work.

We still face temptation, though, and confronting temptations about values, personal sources of power, and how we will fulfill God's plan for our lives is something each of us must do. We constantly receive grace from God to help us respond to sinful temptations and to be as faithful to God as Jesus was.

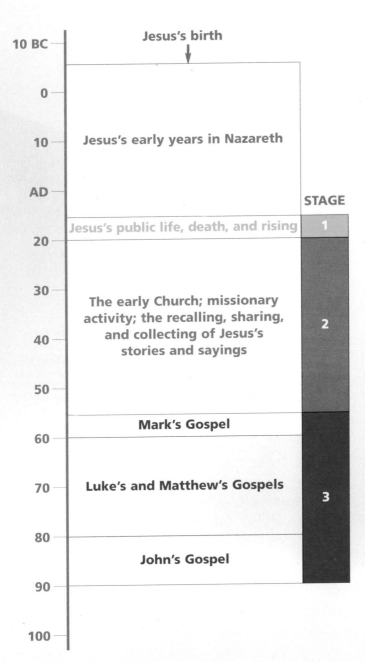

10 BC	**Jesus's birth**
0	
10	**Jesus's early years in Nazareth**
AD	**STAGE**
	Jesus's public life, death, and rising — **1**
20	
30	**The early Church; missionary activity; the recalling, sharing, and collecting of Jesus's stories and sayings** — **2**
40	
50	
60	**Mark's Gospel**
70	**Luke's and Matthew's Gospels** — **3**
80	
	John's Gospel
90	
100	

The *Magnificat* of Mary

"My soul magnifies the Lord,
    and my spirit rejoices in God my
        Savior,
for he has looked with favor on the
        lowliness of his servant.
    Surely, from now on all generations
        will call me blessed;
for the Mighty One has done great
        things for me,
    and holy is his name.
His mercy is for those who fear him
        from generation to generation.
He has shown strength with his arm;
    he has scattered the proud in the
        thoughts of their hearts.
He has brought down the powerful
        from their thrones,
    and lifted up the lowly;
He has filled the hungry with good
        things,
    and sent the rich away empty.
He has helped his servant Israel,
    in remembrance of his mercy,
according to the promise he made to
        our ancestors,
    to Abraham and to his
        descendants forever."

—Luke 1:46–55

Called to the desert

All followers of Jesus will at times experience their own "desert," times when they struggle to find meaning and wrestle with the values that will guide their lives. What are the ways young people today are tempted to find security, meaning, or purpose through economic power? through personal power? through political power, that is, power that comes from having a leadership role or position?

The Role of Mary

During the first several hundred years of the Church's history, Church leaders debated how best to describe Mary's role. Some argued that Mary could not be given the title "Mother of God" because, among other reasons, a human could not possibly generate a divine being. However, others argued that if Jesus was truly human and divine, then Mary should rightly be called Mother of God because she carried him in her womb and gave birth to him. (The familiar title "Mother of God" is a translation of a Greek word, *Theotokos,* meaning "God bearer.") A Church council (an official gathering of leaders) held in the fifth century officially affirmed that Mary is truly "Mother of God." The council's statement about Mary was also a re-affirmation of Jesus's identity as both God and man.

Catholics have always honored Mary as being especially favored by God. One way they do this is by celebrating special holy days each year: the Solemnity of Mary, the Mother of God, January 1; the Assumption of the Blessed Virgin Mary, August 15; and the Immaculate Conception, December 8. Catholics also pray special prayers and devotions that recognize Mary's place of honor, such as the Hail Mary; the Hail, Holy Queen; the Memorare; the rosary; and the Litany of the Blessed Virgin Mary. In addition, shrines have been established at locations such as Lourdes, Fátima, and Guadalupe—places where Mary is believed by some to have appeared to individuals.

Some people believe that Catholics "worship" Mary as if she were a god. However, that is a false understanding of the high esteem in which Catholics hold Mary. Catholics recognize in Mary not a god or a goddess, but a human being who has received abundant blessings from God and who stands as the greatest model of what we strive to become—persons with total faith in the promises of God. In that sense she is the model for all who claim to be disciples of Jesus.

The Reign of God: Jesus's Mission

Jesus said to [the blind men], "Do you believe that I am able to do this?" They said to him, "Yes, Lord." Then he touched their eyes and said, "According to your faith let it be done to you." And their eyes were opened.

—Matthew 9:28–30

Central to Jesus's identity, his life, his mission and message, and all his words and actions is the notion of the Kingdom, or Reign, of God. Jesus's parables proclaim and describe the Kingdom, and his miracles are signs of the Kingdom's presence in the people's midst. Therefore we have to understand what Jesus meant by the Kingdom of God if we are to understand him.

How Did Jesus Understand the Kingdom of God?

Jesus taught that the Kingdom of God was the reign of God's love over the hearts of people and, as a result, a new social order of "righteousness and peace and joy in the Holy Spirit" (Romans 14:17). "By his word, through signs that manifest the reign of God, and by sending out his disciples," Jesus called all people to union with him, to enter the kingdom of God (*Catechism*, no. 542). "To enter it, one must first accept Jesus's word" (*Catechism*, no. 543).

According to Jesus, the Kingdom of God was not to be established through the military overthrow of political oppressors. God would establish it as people came to recognize God's Reign over their heart and life and began to live as true brothers and sisters. When Jesus said that "'the kingdom of God has come near'" (Mark 1:15), he was saying that because of his own unique relationship with God and his profound love of all people—even his enemies. He was himself establishing the Kingdom among people. As a result, those who would eventually witness Jesus's death and Resurrection would recognize him as the One they had been waiting for—their Messiah.

The Church and the Kingdom of God

The Church is the seed and the beginning of the Kingdom of God. Jesus proclaims the Kingdom as already and not yet, a present and future reality. God's Reign is present in the world but not yet fully realized. God's Reign is also present in the Church, but not in all its fullness. It is an error to assume that the Kingdom is something that will come into existence only in heaven, when life on Earth is over. Likewise, it is a mistake to believe that we can create the fullness of God's Reign here on Earth. We are, however, called to live toward the fulfillment of God's Reign, in other words, to participate by doing our part as children of God.

The Church's mission is to proclaim God's Reign, to cooperate with God's plan to establish the Kingdom among all people, and to serve as the seed of the Kingdom. That happens whenever and wherever the love of God is lived out, whenever and wherever the will of God is fulfilled. All people are called to belong to the People of God—to form a community transformed by the Holy Spirit into a people of faith, hope, and love, and to be witnesses of the presence of the Kingdom to the world. Because of the influence of sin, however, the Kingdom of God will never be fully realized on Earth. We wait with hope for God's will to be fulfilled, and we continue to pray with Jesus Christ, "thy kingdom come."

Catechism quote Jesus's invitation to enter his kingdom comes in the form of parables, a characteristic feature of his teaching.[5] Through his parables he invites people to the feast of the kingdom, but he also asks for a radical choice: to gain the kingdom, one must give everything.[6] Words are not enough; deeds are required.[7]

—*Catechism*, no. 546

Bible byte **The Beatitudes:**
Characteristics of a Kingdom People

When Jesus saw the crowds, he went up the mountain; and after he sat down, his disciples came to him. Then he began to speak, and taught them, saying:

"Blessed are the poor in spirit, for theirs is the kingdom of heaven.

"Blessed are those who mourn, for they will be comforted.

"Blessed are the meek, for they will inherit the earth.

"Blessed are those who hunger and thirst for righteousness, for they will be filled.

"Blessed are the merciful, for they will receive mercy.

"Blessed are the pure in heart, for they will see God.

"Blessed are the peacemakers, for they will be called children of God.

"Blessed are those who are persecuted for righteousness' sake, for theirs is the kingdom of heaven.

"Blessed are you when people revile you and persecute you and utter all kinds of evil against you falsely on my account. Rejoice and be glad, for your reward is great in heaven, for in the same way they persecuted the prophets who were before you."

—Matthew 5:1–12

The Good News proclaimed to me

Jesus proclaimed that in and through him, healing was available for people in painful situations. In Luke 4:16–23 (see also Isaiah 61:1–2), Jesus's message is clear: Poor people will hear good news; brokenhearted people will have their brokenness mended; people who have been blind will recover their sight; people in captivity will experience liberation; and people in mourning will find comfort. Of these five promises Jesus made, which one speaks most to your heart and life right now? In what area of your life do you most need healing?

Parables and Miracles:
Jesus Teaches and Heals

Two important characteristics of Jesus, those of a teacher and a healer, are central to the Gospel message. An investigation of these characteristics will add to the knowledge about Jesus that we are seeking as we prepare for Confirmation.

Jesus the Teacher

The title teacher as a direct reference to Jesus is used in the Gospels at least thirty times. Here are some key points to keep in mind regarding the style and content of Jesus's teaching:

> Virtually all Jesus's teaching related in one way or another to his proclamation of the Kingdom of God.

> Most of the other respected Jewish teachers of Jesus's day (called rabbis) backed up everything they said by referring to the Scriptures and to the teachings of other respected rabbis. But Jesus often indicated that he was the sole judge of the truth of what he taught.

> Jesus had a unique relationship with his disciples. Normally disciples chose a rabbi to learn from. Jesus, however, chose his own disciples, and he called them into a lasting relationship with him.

> One of the most striking features of Jesus's teaching was his use of parables. The word *parable* comes from a word meaning "comparison." Using everyday situations Jesus would commonly compare the Kingdom of God to another reality—for example, a mustard seed, yeast in bread, or a sower in a field. Jesus would often add a surprising twist to his stories, something that would catch his listeners off guard and make a strong impression on them.

Jesus the Healer

Perhaps no image of Jesus intrigues us more than Jesus as "the miracle worker." Our imagination is caught up with the scenes of power and awe—people raised to life with a simple word, blindness cured with a touch, sickness and disease rendered powerless in the presence of Jesus's power.

Heart link [Jesus] was a human being so close to his God that God's own creative power flowed out of him in healing waves. He was a man so dedicated to God's work that his own fascinating power seemed to embarass him; at times it seemed even to get in the way of his message. But most of all, Jesus was a man so charged with God's own compassion and love that any cry of pain or confusion drew from him an instant response of healing and restoration.

—Donald Senior

 Bible byte When John [the Baptist] heard in prison what the Messiah was doing, he sent word by his disciples and said to him, "Are you the one who is to come, or are we to wait for another?" Jesus answered them, "Go and tell John what you hear and see: the blind receive their sight, the lame walk, the lepers are cleansed, the deaf hear, the dead are raised, and the poor have good news brought to them. And blessed is anyone who takes no offense at me."

—Matthew 11:2–6

"Everyone then who hears these words of mine and acts on them will be like a wise man who built his house on rock. The rain fell, the floods came, and the winds blew and beat on that house, but it did not fall, because it had been founded on rock. . . ."

Now when Jesus had finished saying these things, the crowds were astounded at his teaching, for he taught them as one having authority, and not as their scribes.

—Matthew 7:24–29

Bear with one another and, if anyone has a complaint against another, forgive each other; just as the Lord has forgiven you, so you also must forgive.

—Colossians 3:13

Jesus's miracles are signs of the powerful, loving presence of God in the world. They show that Jesus is divine, truly the Son of God, the promised Messiah. The miraculous events helped those who walked with him realize that Jesus Christ and God's Kingdom are linked—you cannot have one without the other. Jesus says, "Even though you do not believe me, believe the works, so that you may know and understand that the Father is in me and I am in the Father" (John 10:38).

Here are the kinds of miracles that can be found in the Gospels:

> *Healing miracles.* Jesus relieved the physical suffering of people afflicted with fever, paralysis, deafness, muteness, blindness, and "leprosy" (a general name given to many kinds of skin disorders of Jesus's day).

> *Exorcisms.* Evil spirits or demons were driven out of people at Jesus's command.

> *Restorations of life.* On three occasions Jesus conquered death itself by "raising people from the dead."

> *Nature miracles.* Jesus demonstrated apparent control over the natural world by walking on water, calming a storm, feeding thousands with just a few loaves and fishes, and so on.

The miracles worked by Jesus are signs that attest that God the Father has sent him. Those who witness or hear of such miracles are invited to believe in him, and "those who turn to him in faith, he grants what they ask"[8] (*Catechism,* number 548). We hear in the Scriptures of miracles performed by Jesus that free people from the evils of hunger, injustice, illness, and death. These miracles are messianic signs—they testify that God the Father sent his son, Jesus, to free us from sin, which impedes us in our love of God and neighbor. (Adapted from *Catechism,* numbers 548, 549). Often our modern minds want scientific proof of why things happen, but scientific proof does not explain the mystery of a miracle. The grace of an open heart and a willingness to place our trust in something we don't understand can help us grow into a deeper appreciation and understanding of miracles. Miracles aren't "hocus pocus"; they are rooted in love and the mercy of God.

Jesus' Parables in the Gospels of Matthew, Mark, and Luke

	Matthew	Mark	Luke
The house built on rock	7:24–27	8:4–15	
The sower	13:1–23	4:1–20	
The weeds among the wheat	13:24–30,36–43	13:18–19	
The mustard seed	13:31–32	4:30–32	
The hidden treasure and the pearls	13:44–46		
The unforgiving servant	18:23–35		
The good Samaritan			10:25–37
The rich fool			12:16–21
The great feast			14:15–24
The lost sheep	18:12–14		15:4–7
The lost coin			15:8–10
The prodigal son			15:11–32
The unjust servant			16:1–13
The rich man and Lazarus			16:19–31
The unjust judge			18:1–8
The Pharisee and the tax collector			18:9–14
The laborers in the vineyard	20:1–16		
The wicked tenants	21:33–44	12:1–12	20:9–18
The wedding banquet	22:1–14		
The faithful servant	24:45–51		
The ten bridesmaids	25:1–13		
The talents or sums of money	25:14–30		19:11–27

Jesus' Miracles in the Gospels of Matthew, Mark, and Luke

	Matthew	Mark	Luke
Cleansing a leper	8:1–4	1:40–45	5:12–16
Healing a centurion's servant	8:5–13		7:1–10
Curing Peter's mother-in-law	8:14–15	1:29–31	4:38–39
Calming a storm	8:23–27	4:35–41	8:22–25
Healing the Gadarene demoniac(s)	8:28–34	5:1–20	8:26–39
Healing a paralytic	9:1–8	2:1–12	5:17–26
Jairus's daughter and the woman with a hemorrhage	9:18–26	5:21–43	8:40–56
Healing two blind men	9:27–31		
The man with a withered hand	12:9–14	3:1–6	6:6–11
First miracle of the loaves	14:13–21	6:30–44	9:10–17
Raising the widow's son			7:11–17
Walking on water	14:22–33	6:45–52	
Curing the Canaanite woman's daughter	15:21–28	7:24–30	
Healing a deaf man			7:31–37
Second miracle of the loaves	15:32–39	8:1–10	
The blind man of Bethsaida		8:22–26	
Healing a boy who has a demon	17:14–20	9:14–29	9:37–42
Cleansing ten lepers			17:11–19
Healing blindness at Jericho	20:29–34	10:46–52	18:35–43
The barren fig tree	21:18–22		

Bible byte Let love be genuine; hate what is evil, hold fast to what is good; love one another with mutual affection; outdo one another in showing honor. Do not lag in zeal, be ardent in spirit, serve the Lord. Rejoice in hope, be patient in suffering, persevere in prayer. Contribute to the needs of the saints; extend hospitality to strangers.

Bless those who persecute you; bless and do not curse them. . . . Do not be overcome by evil, but overcome evil with good.

—Romans 12:9–14,21

What do you want me to do for you?

In Mark's Gospel Jesus asks a blind man named Bartimaeus, "What do you want me to do for you?" Bartimaeus answers with a response that perhaps every believer frequently feels and should often pray: "Master, I want to see." If Jesus now asked you, "What do you want me to do for you?" how would you answer him? What kind of "sight" do you need in your life right now?

Sin: An Obstacle to the Reign of God

Experience teaches us that there is a dark side to life. Though grace may draw us toward God, our freedom allows us to disobey him. So sin is as much a part of our life as grace. Despite our ability to achieve heroic acts of love, we are quite capable of willful selfishness. And along with our capacity to help heal the wounds of others through compassion and tenderness, we are also capable of inflicting wounds on one another. We make a mistake if we overstate our own goodness and ignore our need for God's powerful gift of forgiveness whenever we sin. The joy and happiness we desire are not rooted in our achievements or in accomplishing the unrealistic goal of perfection in this life. True happiness comes from rejecting sin and turning to God, who is the source of all goodness and love.

Sin: It's About Relationships, Not Just Rules

Sin exists. As the *Catechism* asserts, "Sin is present in human history; any attempt to ignore it or to give this dark reality other names would be futile" (number 386).

Sins are the things we deliberately think, say, do, or fail to do that are contrary to the eternal law of God. They offend God and defy reason. Sin is, simply put, anything that violates the will of God. The Scriptures and Tradition reveal clearly that the will of God is all about relationships—relationships between God and people, between individual persons, between groups of people, and between people and the rest of the created world. Therefore, sin is anything that corrupts or ruptures the kinds of relationships desired by God. "To try to understand what sin is, one must first recognize the profound relation of man to God, for only in this relationship is the evil of sin unmasked in its true identity as humanity's rejection of God and opposition to him" (*Catechism,* number 386). Further, "sin is an abuse of the freedom that God gives to created persons so that they are capable of loving him and loving one another" (number 387).

Bible byte For just as by the one man's disobedience [Adam] the many were made sinners, so by the one man's obedience [Jesus Christ] the many will be made righteous. . . . As sin exercised dominion in death, so grace might also exercise dominion through justification leading to eternal life through Jesus Christ our Lord.

—Romans 5:19–21

Negative Cultural Values: Learning to Fight Back

Our contemporary culture is deeply influenced by a variety of negative values that jeopardize the kind of relationships God desires for us. These are so pervasive that we all have a difficult time avoiding their impact. Four such values seem particularly influential among people of all ages in our society:

> **Excessive consumerism.** Excessive consumerism is the cultural drive to acquire more and more goods, many of which are totally unnecessary, while much of the world goes without necessities.

> **Extreme individualism.** Extreme individualism is individuality (which can be good) stressed to the point that we lose all sense of responsibility to others. Service to others is replaced with the belief that we must take care of ourselves first. The sense of the common good is lost.

> **Immediate gratification.** Immediate gratification is the basis for the conviction, "If it feels good, do it." We want and expect all our needs to be met right now, not tomorrow, and certainly not in a few years.

> **Sexual permissiveness.** Sexual permissiveness is the approach to sexuality that results from the other negative cultural values defined above. People are viewed as products to be consumed. The desire for individual freedom leads to the inability to commit to marriage, and the desire for immediate gratification leads to recreational sexual activity outside the bonds of marriage without concern for the physical, emotional, or spiritual harm it can cause. These cultural values stand in stark contrast to God's law of love. They promote sin that is gravely contrary to the chaste life we are called to live (see *Catechism*, number 2396). They shun the reality that a man and a woman in marriage form an intimate communion of life and love, a union which "by its very nature . . . is ordered to the good of the couple, as well as to the generation . . . of children" (number 1660).

Jesus, in his teaching and actions, contradicted each one of these cultural values:

> Our culture asks, How can I acquire lots of things? Jesus asks, How can I share what I have with others?

> Our culture asks, How can I remain totally independent? Jesus asks, How can I help bring people together?

Act of Contrition (Sorrow)

My God,
I am sorry for my sins with all my
    heart, and I detest them.
In choosing to do wrong and failing
    to do good,
I have sinned against you, whom I
    should love above all things.
I firmly intend, with your help,
    to do penance, to sin no more,
and to avoid whatever leads me
    to sin.
Our Savior Jesus Christ suffered and
    died for us.
In his name, my God, have mercy.
                Amen.

> Our culture asks, How can I make my life easy right now? Jesus says, I may have to lose my life now in order ultimately to save it.

Adam, Eve, and Original Sin

The Book of Genesis in the Old Testament tells the story of Adam and Eve and their fall from grace. God created them in a perfect state of holiness and justice, symbolized by their life of happiness in the Garden of Eden. They did not suffer and would never have to experience death. They enjoyed profound intimacy with God.

All this came to an end when they disobeyed God and committed the first sin. They gave in to the serpent's temptation to eat the fruit God specifically commanded them not to eat. Adam and Eve and all people born after them would suffer the consequences of their sinful disobedience.

This story is figurative, which means it is not a literal historical account. The story does, however, convey a truth. By sinning, our first parents introduced suffering and evil into the world. The Church's doctrine of original sin expresses the consequences of this. Everyone is born with a wounded human nature, deprived of the full holiness and justice that God intended for every person. It doesn't mean that human beings have lost their goodness or that God is not with us. Rather, it means that our lives are affected by ignorance, suffering, and the threat of death, and that we are inclined toward sin. Our relationships with God, one another, and creation lack the harmony that God desires. How this sin is transmitted is a mystery we cannot fully grasp.

The "reverse side" of the doctrine of original sin is the Good News that Jesus Christ offers everyone salvation and makes a new life possible!

Kinds of Sin

Catholics use a variety of terms to identify the multiple meanings and human expressions of sin. Here are the most common ones:

> **Original sin** is the sin of Adam and Eve, who disobeyed God; and the fallen state of human nature, which separates every person from him as a result of Adam and Eve's first act of disobedience and through which sin became universally present in the world. Christ came to offer himself to save all humanity from this universal dominion of sin.

> **Venial sin** is a less serious offense against the will of God that diminishes one's personal character and weakens but does not rupture one's relationship with him.

> **Mortal sin** is an action so contrary to the will of God that it results in a complete separation from him and his grace. As a consequence of that separation, the person is condemned to eternal death. To be a mortal sin requires three conditions: it must involve grave matter, a person must have full knowledge of the evil of the act, and a person must give her or his full consent in committing the act.

> **Social sin** is the collective effect of sin over time, which corrupts society and its institutions by creating "structures of sin." Examples are racism, sexism, and institutionalized poverty.

Bible Bytes After he had washed their feet, . . . [Jesus] said to [his disciples], "Do you know what I have done to you? . . . I have set you an example that you also should do as I have done to you."

—John 13:12–15

Facing my dark side

In his Letter to the Romans, Saint Paul talks about his constant struggle against the weaknesses he experiences in himself. "What a lousy person I am!" he says. And then he pleads, "Who can possibly save me from the mess I'm in?" (see Romans 7:15–25).

In the space provided, write about a time in your life—perhaps even now—when you felt as Paul did. Close your reflections by asking God to help you in your struggle.

Jesus Rejected: The Meaning of the Cross

It was probably around the year 30, according to our calendar. Jesus was only a little more than thirty years old, and his life was about to end abruptly and violently. He had preached for no more than three years. He had proclaimed the Good News about a kingdom of love, joy, peace, and harmony. But it had all led to this—the road to the cross. Yet God was in fact saving humanity through his Son's violent death. How can that be?

To answer that question, it is helpful to consider two perspectives. The first perspective is the religious and political conflicts that led to Jesus's Crucifixion. The second and most important perspective is what the Holy Spirit has revealed about the meaning of Jesus Christ's death for the salvation of the human race.

Why It Happened: A Man of Peace, a Source of Conflict

Certainly Jesus was committed to peace, and we are right to remember most strongly his acts of love and compassion. But we must remember as well that he seemed to cause conflict and tension wherever he went. His words were often challenging, even threatening, to his listeners. His behavior often shocked those who witnessed it, for it ran contrary to many of the accepted practices of the time. Consider the following points:

> On virtually every important issue of his day—marriage, authority, the role and meaning of the Law, the Temple, worship—Jesus's teachings conflicted with those of people in positions of power.

> Jesus made the outcasts of society—women, poor people, tax collectors, sinners, those who were physically or mentally ill—the very cornerstone of his message about God's Kingdom. His demand for justice threatened all those who would cling to their own privilege, power, and possessions.

> Jesus spoke with an authority superior to the religious and political powers of his day. This came to a head when he reclaimed the Temple as a place of prayer and devotion to God (see Mark 11:15–19). His actions brought him to a direct and unavoidable confrontation with the Jewish and Roman authorities. He was a very real threat to religious tradition and political stability. So, on a strict-

ly human and historical level, Jesus's violent end was the price he paid for living a life of love, justice, and commitment to his heavenly Father. For Jesus, the Son of God, to live otherwise would be a betrayal of his very being. The historical event of Jesus's death is significant because he was not just a man willing to die for his beliefs. Because he is the Son of God, Jesus's death has a larger, more profound meaning.

The Eucharist: "This Is My Body, Given for You"

The Eucharist, or Mass, is the central saving act for Catholics, the core of the Church's life. The Mass recalls Jesus Christ's sacrificial gift of himself on the cross and makes the power of Jesus's dying and rising present to us today.

When we celebrate the Eucharist, we break bread as Jesus did at the Last Supper, in memory of him. We recognize that Jesus himself is present with us in the form of the bread and wine—that the consecrated bread is the body of Jesus broken for us, and the consecrated wine is the blood of Jesus poured out for us. This mystery in which the bread and wine is changed into the body and blood of Christ is called transubstantiation. In sharing Christ's body and blood, we proclaim that Jesus's sacrifice of love is with us now and forever. We are united in Christ with the love of God through the Holy Spirit and with one another. This is the great meaning of the Eucharist, which literally means "thanksgiving."

The Gospel Story of the Passion and Death of Jesus

The arrest, trial, and Crucifixion of Jesus are the most extensively reported events in the Gospels. It should not surprise us to learn that the Passion narratives in the Gospels differ somewhat from one another. By reviewing all the Gospel accounts together, we can get a general idea of the unfolding events that led up to Jesus's death:

> **The Last Supper.** Jesus served as host for a special meal for his disciples, and he followed some of the normal customs for such a role. Jesus's words and actions were packed with meaning about his approaching death and its connection with this meal. The Last Supper marks the creation and institution of the Eucharist, or Mass, at which the risen Christ is truly present.

It was now about noon, and darkness came over the whole land until three in the afternoon, while the sun's light failed; and the curtain of the temple was torn in two. Then Jesus, crying with a loud voice, said, "Father, into your hands I commend my spirit." Having said this, he breathed his last. When the centurion saw what had taken place, he praised God and said, "Certainly this man was innocent." And when all the crowds who had gathered there for this spectacle saw what had taken place, they returned home, beating their breasts. But all his acquaintances, including the women who had followed him from Galilee, stood at a distance, watching these things.

—Luke 23:44–49

In many ways Jesus's violent end was the price he paid for living a life of love, justice, and commitment to the One who sent him.

> **The agony in the garden.** In the garden at Gethsemane, shortly before his arrest, Jesus told his disciples that he was deeply grieved. He threw himself on the ground and prayed, "My Father, if it is possible, let this cup pass from me" (Matthew 26:39). He expressed the horror of the suffering and death he would soon face, but he accepted the Father's will that he die in order to redeem us.

> **The trial and appearance before Pilate.** Jesus appeared before the Great Sanhedrin, where the Jewish leaders tried to decide what charge to level against him. They decided to charge him with blasphemy, because of Jesus's apparent claim of equality with God. The Jews needed the Roman rulers to carry out a death penalty—hence the need for Pilate, the Roman governor. Pilate ordered Jesus to be executed based on the official Roman charge that Jesus had claimed to be the King of the Jews.

> **The scourging and Crucifixion.** Jesus was brutally beaten and then forced to make the painful walk (often referred to as the Way of the Cross) to his execution by crucifixion.

> **"Into your hands . . ."** Jesus died remaining faithful to his Father. Some Gospel accounts even portray his forgiveness for those who killed him and his ultimate trust in his Father, the one he called "Abba."

The Meaning of the Cross

The Church teaches the meaning of Jesus's death and how it is the means for our salvation in varied language and images.

Jesus, the Suffering Servant

Christ's suffering on the cross and Resurrection stands at the center of the Good News proclaimed by the Apostles, and the Church following them. "God's saving plan was accomplished 'once and for all' by the redemptive death of his Son Jesus Christ" (*Catechism,* number 571).

Jesus, the Paschal Lamb

The Evangelist John linked the death of Jesus with the killing of the paschal lambs, who were slaughtered as part of the Jewish celebration of Passover. During the first Passover, the blood of lambs was a sign that spared the Israelites from death and led to their liberation from slavery. By using this imagery, John revealed that Jesus's death saved us, and continues to save us even today, from slavery to sin. You might recall these familiar words from the Mass: "Behold the Lamb of God, behold him who takes away the sin of the world."

Jesus, a Ransom for Many

Many of the early believers were Gentiles who would not understand Jewish images and understandings of Jesus's death. In the Roman world, a ransom was paid to release a slave, and someone other than the slave often paid it. Mark, who was writing for a Gentile audience, borrowed this imagery and referred to Jesus as one who "came not to be served but to serve, and to give his life [as] a ransom for many" (10:45). Again, we see here the image of Jesus's death as one that frees believers from slavery to sin.

"Jesus Died for Our Sins"

Ultimately all these images and metaphors express a common truth: God the Father loved us and sent his son, Jesus Christ, to free us from sin and to reconcile us to himself. Jesus freely offered himself for our salvation, and through his death, he atoned, or made amends, for the sins of all humankind. He bridged the separation between God and humanity caused by sin and made it possible for all people to attain communion with God. Jesus Christ accomplished the redemption of humankind because through his divinity, he was in some way able to unite himself to all people.

At the core of the Crucifixion, and therefore at the very heart of the Catholic faith, is this truth: Through the Death and Resurrection of Jesus, God poured out unlimited, complete love for all people. The cross ultimately becomes a sign of how much God loves us.

The fact is, however, that the death of Jesus cannot be fully understood until we understand what followed it—Jesus's Resurrection from the dead. None of the Gospels ends with Jesus's Passion and death on the cross. Rather, each Gospel proclaims that Jesus is alive. He is risen from the dead!

 Whether our pain and difficulties are freely chosen or thrust upon us, we have some choice about how we respond. We have freedom to shape meaning, to find purpose as we bear our struggles. And as Christians, we have a model.

—Mary Ellen Ashcroft and Holly Bridges

Here Lies . . . Me

The Stations of the Cross

The stations of the cross is a Catholic devotion that commemorates the Passion of Jesus. The practice began, most likely, in Jerusalem soon after Jesus's death. Believers prayerfully processed along the route that Jesus walked from his trial before Pilate to the cross on Calvary, stopping along the way for prayer and reflection at key places, or stations.

During the Middle Ages, the devotion spread and became more formalized. The design of most Catholic churches from that time on included the stations, often represented along the walls in forms ranging from simple crosses to highly detailed paintings or sculptures.

In Catholic churches today, the stations are most commonly practiced during the season of Lent, usually on Fridays. The fourteen traditional stations are listed below:

1. Jesus is condemned to death.

2. Jesus bears the cross.

3. Jesus falls the first time.

4. Jesus meets his mother.

5. Simon of Cyrene helps Jesus carry his cross.

6. Veronica wipes the face of Jesus.

7. Jesus falls a second time.

8. Jesus meets the women of Jerusalem.

9. Jesus falls a third time.

10. Jesus is stripped of his garments.

11. Jesus is nailed to the cross.

12. Jesus dies on the cross.

13. Jesus is taken down from the cross.

14. Jesus is placed in the tomb.

Bible byte [Before he ascended into heaven, Jesus said to them], "All authority in heaven and on earth has been given to me. Go therefore and make disciples of all nations. . . . And remember, I am with you always, to the end of the age."

—Matthew 28:18–20

Catechism quote The Paschal mystery of Christ's cross and Resurrection stands at the center of the Good News that the apostles, and the Church following them, are to proclaim to the world. God's saving plan was accomplished "once and for all"[9] by the redemptive death of his Son Jesus Christ.

—*Catechism*, no. 571

A matter of life and death

We frequently hear that "Jesus died for us" or that "we are saved by the blood of the cross." What meaning does Jesus's death hold for you? How do you understand what it means to be saved by Jesus's death on the cross? Feel free to write whatever comes to your mind or heart in response to these questions.

The Resurrection: God Is Victorious!

None of the Gospels ends with Jesus's Passion and death on the cross. The Gospels themselves—indeed, Christianity as a recognized religion—would not even exist were it not for the event that took place after the death of Jesus. The last days of Jesus's earthly life—his arrest, trial, and death by crucifixion—have been recalled and passed on for some two thousand years. The Resurrection manifested their meaning, confirming the truth of Jesus's divinity, making new life in the Holy Spirit possible for us.

Curiously, the Gospel accounts of the Resurrection of Jesus are brief compared with those of the final days of Jesus's life. The accounts of the event found in the Gospels are surprisingly straightforward, offer little detail, and make no attempt to further explain what happened.

What's the Big Deal?

Most people occasionally wonder about their own death, the fact that their life, as they now know and experience it, will eventually come to an end. The Resurrection of Jesus means that those who believe in him and his promises can trust that they, too, will experience life after their own death.

We experience the reality of death not only in the actual loss of life. We each experience at least hints of the reality of death in many other "death moments" in our life: the times when we feel lonely and isolated, separated or alienated from those we love and care for, moments when our minds are filled with confusion and uncertainty. All those experiences can remind us of and point us toward the ultimate mystery of death. All those experiences also can fill our life with a real sense of darkness.

However, as Catholics we are a people who claim love, joy, and peace as our hallmarks. We constantly claim to find hope amid all the suffering in our life and in the world as a whole. How can this be? What can make sense of this? Ultimately, the foundation for everything we believe, do, and are as Catholics is the event that followed the death of Jesus—his Resurrection. Without the Resurrection, Saint Paul tells us, "then our proclamation has been in vain and your faith has been in vain. . . . If for this life only we have hoped in Christ, we are of all people most to be pitied" (1 Corinthians 15:14,19). Without the Resurrection of Jesus, death wins. This implies not only the victory of physical death over the power of life but also the victory

Bible byte You yourselves are our letter, written on our hearts, to be known and read by all; and you show that you are a letter of Christ, prepared by us, written not with ink but with the Spirit of the living God, not on tablets of stone but on tablets of human hearts.

—2 Corinthians 3:2–3

of all those other "death moments" of difficulty, confusion, loneliness, and despair. Yet in the Resurrection of Jesus, we discover the marvelous truth that life is stronger than death, that goodness ultimately conquers evil, that hatred can be overcome by love, and that our life can be filled with a kind of light that removes all darkness.

Bible byte

"See, the home of God is among mortals.
He will dwell with them;
they will be his peoples,
and God himself will be with them;
he will wipe away every tear from
    their eyes.
Death will be no more;
mourning and crying and pain
    will be no more,
for the first things have
    passed away."

—Revelation 21:3–4

A Promise of Everlasting Life

Catholic Connection Catholics recite the creed at Mass; listen to this line from the Nicene Creed: "We look for the resurrection of the dead, and the life of the world to come." Then we say, "Amen," which means, "Yes!" Amen comes from a Hebrew word that means "trustworthiness and faithfulness." Our amen is a recognition of God's faithfulness toward us and an expression of our belief and trust.

Paul VI said, "We believe that the souls of all who die in Christ's grace . . . are the People of God beyond death"—not just our spirit or soul will go on after our death (see *Catechism,* number 1052). "On the last day" (John 6:40)—that is, at the end of the world—all who have died in union with God will be united with their glorified body. How will this happen? What will our glorified body look like? As the Catechism says, the answer to such questions "exceeds our imagination and understanding; it is accessible only to faith" (number 1000). But the belief, the reality, the fact, of life after death "has been an essential element of the Christian faith from its beginnings" (number 991). And to that we can only say, "Amen, indeed! Yes!"

The Gospel Accounts of the Resurrection and Ascension of Jesus

The Resurrection of Jesus and his Ascension (the name given to his passage out of earthly existence and into the presence of his Father) are recorded in the Gospels in straightforward, simple language. We find little of the kind of detailed description that characterizes the accounts of his trial and execution. This may be because the Resurrection and Ascension are quite literally "too big for words." But here are several points that bear special mention regarding these marvelous events:

> ▶ *The Resurrection is real.* Though the Gospel stories of the Resurrection differ in some descriptive points, the Resurrection of Jesus is real.

- *Jesus's disciples were transformed by it.* The disciples, in hiding since Jesus's Crucifixion, were converted into a community of such strong believers that they radically altered the course of history. Two thousand years later, we are still transformed by what happened on that day.

- *In the Ascension, Jesus did not "go away."* He is now present among us in a new and different way, through the presence of the Holy Spirit.

- *Jesus is alive among and within us.* The Resurrection and Ascension together mean that Jesus has moved beyond the limits of time and space and fully into the presence of his Father.

What Does the Resurrection Tell Us About Jesus?

What does the Resurrection tell us about Jesus and his mission? The Resurrection confirms that Jesus Christ is the Son of God, the Word made flesh, sent by God the Father to redeem the world. He is the Messiah, the Christ, the Lord of the universe.

For the first disciples, seeing the resurrected Jesus was clear proof that Jesus was more than just another human being. The story of doubting Thomas says it most clearly. When Thomas sees the resurrected Jesus for the first time, he declares, "My Lord and my God!" (John 20:28). Belief in Jesus's Resurrection and belief in the Incarnation go hand in hand. Throughout the centuries people have believed in the divinity of Jesus Christ because they first believed in his Resurrection.

The Resurrection reveals the Son of God's oneness with his Father through the power of the Holy Spirit.

- In his teaching about God's unconditional love for us, Jesus spoke the truth.

- In his promise that we find our fulfillment in loving God and others, Jesus spoke the truth.

- In his rejection of hollow and empty rituals and in his unity through prayer with the Father, Jesus spoke the truth.

- In his conviction that forgiveness of one another will always be more life giving and enriching than revenge, Jesus spoke the truth.

Catechism quote The Church has no other light than Christ's; according to a favorite image of the Church Fathers, the Church is like the moon, all its light reflected from the sun.

—*Catechism*, no. 748

> In his call for respect and compassion for the outcasts of society, Jesus spoke the truth.

> In his teaching that rich people must share with poor people, Jesus spoke the truth.

> In his absolute refusal to accept the human-made prejudices that separate us from one another, Jesus spoke the truth.

The Paschal Mystery

The mystery of Christ's life, death, and Resurrection and our redemption through those events is sometimes referred to as the Paschal mystery. Paschal comes from the Greek word *pascha,* meaning "passover." Jesus passed over from death to new life. The New Testament refers to Jesus as the "Lamb of God" and the "Paschal Lamb." Just as the blood of a slain lamb spared the lives of the Israelites and led to their release from captivity in Egypt, now the death of Jesus frees us from sin and death. Because of Jesus we are able to participate in this passing over to a new life in the Holy Spirit. The Church's liturgies celebrate above all the salvation Christ accomplished for us through the Paschal mystery of his dying and rising. Furthermore, his death and Resurrection are made present through the liturgy of the Church.

We will experience the fullness of this new life only after death. In the meantime, however, we can see glimpses of the Paschal mystery. Throughout our life we experience big and little "deaths" in a variety of ways: through the suffering caused by illness, the emotional loss of a good friend who moves away, the heartache of failing to make the team, or the anger and hurt caused by divorce. The Paschal mystery promises that God can make something life giving come out of our pain and loss. If you listen to faithful Christians for a while, you will hear story after story about how God helped them see or experience something good and wonderful during difficult times.

From death to Resurrection and new life—the Paschal mystery seems to permeate all of life for those with eyes to see and ears to hear (see Mark 8:18).

The Paschal Triduum

During the days between the end of Lent and the beginning of Easter, Catholic worship focuses in a particular way on the Passion, death, and Resurrection of Jesus. Those key events in Jesus's life are celebrated during three days called the Paschal Triduum (based on the Latin words for "three days"). These special days progress in this way:

> ❯ The Triduum begins with the Mass of the Last Supper on the evening of Holy Thursday.

> ❯ It continues on Good Friday with rituals and Scripture readings that commemorate Jesus's Passion and death.

> ❯ Holy Saturday serves as a day of waiting at Jesus's tomb, a time of special prayerfulness and anticipation of what is to come.

> ❯ The Triduum reaches its crescendo with the Easter Vigil on Saturday evening, a vigil that anticipates and begins the Easter celebration of the Resurrection of Jesus.

> ❯ The Triduum then officially concludes with the celebration of Evening Prayer on Easter Sunday.

The three days of the Paschal Triduum represent the supreme celebration of the entire Catholic liturgical year.

Blessed are those who have not seen but believe

Every Christian at times confronts uncertainty and doubt. Many also experience moments when Jesus seems so real and so present that they want to fall to their knees in recognition of him and exclaim, with Thomas, "My Lord and my God!"

How would you describe your current relationship with Jesus? What doubts or concerns do you have about your faith? What lessons about faith might you learn from the story of Thomas?

Now write here what you think Jesus would say to you in response to your doubts and concerns:

Pentecost: Gift of the Spirit

The period of formation draws to a close with more reflection and discussion on the nature and mission of the Church. The invitation and challenge that this journey toward Confirmation presents to you concerns the Church and your full participation in its life. This session will help you learn more about the Church and your role as a member. It will also give you an opportunity to reflect on how the Holy Spirit is at work in your life.

We learn much about the nature of the Church from the New Testament. In a particularly rich and evocative story, the Evangelist Luke provides wonderful insights. He tells the story of two disciples walking on the road to a village named Emmaus shortly after Jesus has been executed and then raised from the dead (see Luke 24:13–35). The risen Jesus joins them on the road, but they don't realize who he is. Jesus listens sympathetically as they explain what happened during the previous, horrifying days. Christ walks with them in their pain, and then he explains, beginning with Moses and the prophets, what the Scriptures say about the Messiah they awaited.

Send forth your Spirit, and they will be created.

—From Prayer to the Holy Spirit

After some time the disciples invite Jesus to join them for a simple evening meal. During the meal Jesus takes bread and wine as he had done at the Last Supper just a few days earlier. He blesses the bread, breaks it, and hands it to them. The disciples' eyes are opened, and they recognize him. Then Jesus vanishes from their sight. The disciples return to Jerusalem and tell the other disciples and their companions that Jesus has been made known to them in the breaking of the bread.

While the disciples are talking, Jesus appears again. He stands among them and says, "Peace be with you." The disciples, frightened at first, realize who is with them. Before leaving them Jesus tells them that he will be sending what his Father promised, and says, "Stay here in the city until you have been clothed with power from on high" (Luke 24:49). Here is Luke's account of the event that fulfilled this promise:

> When the day of Pentecost had come, they were all together in one place. And suddenly from heaven there came a sound like the rush of a violent wind, and it filled the entire house where they were sitting. Divided tongues, as of fire, appeared among them, and a tongue rested on each of them. All of them were filled with the Holy Spirit and began to speak in other languages, as the

Spirit gave them ability. Now there were devout Jews from every nation under heaven living in Jerusalem. And at this sound the crowd gathered and was bewildered, because each one heard them speaking in the native language of each. Amazed and astonished, they asked, "Are not all these who are speaking Galileans? And how is it that we hear, each of us, in our own native language? . . . All were amazed and perplexed, saying to one another, "What does this mean?" But others sneered and said, "They are filled with new wine."

—Acts of the Apostles 2:1–13

The Scriptures proclaim that Jesus is alive and present, but in a new way. He will no longer walk on Earth as a companion to his disciples in the way he did before the Crucifixion. Instead, he is present through the Holy Spirit. On Pentecost he sent the Spirit to animate the Church and to make it holy. Jesus Christ continues to pour out the Holy Spirit through the Church's celebration of the sacraments. Like the disciples we recognize the presence of the risen Lord in the breaking of the bread—the Eucharist.

The Age of the Church

The outpouring of the Holy Spirit on the day of Pentecost ushered in the "age of the Church." The mission fulfilled by Jesus is carried on by the Church through the power of the Holy Spirit. In other words, the Church, guided by the Holy Spirit, now takes on the responsibility for proclaiming the Good News. Through the presence of the Holy Spirit, the community of believers is empowered to announce—through words and actions—that Christ has conquered sin and death and restored our relationship with the Father. The Spirit nourishes, heals, and organizes the people of God so that all may have life and the ability to use their gifts to bear witness to the Father's love. Jesus speaks to us today just as he spoke to his disciples when he said, "As the Father has sent me, so I send you" (John 20:21).

Though Pentecost is sometimes said to mark the birth of the Church, establishing the Church was God's intention from the beginning of Creation. He created us out of love and wants us to be close to him. The calling together (convocation) of God's people—the Church—is the goal of his plan and the means through which he will accomplish the fullness of the communion he desires to share with us.

What do we mean when we say that the Church is both the means and the goal of God's plan? The Church is the means God uses for fulfilling his plan because the people of the Church witness to Jesus Christ and his message. When Christians practice their love for one another and their compassion for those who are suffering and in need, they are doing so in the name of Christ. When they speak out for justice and advocate for moral issues, they are doing so for Jesus Christ. That witness helps others understand what the love of God is all about and draws them to put their faith in Christ.

But the Church is also the goal of God's plan, because with the aid of the Holy Spirit, the people of the Church live together in such a way as to make the Kingdom of God real in the world. By practicing all the things that Jesus commanded—sacrificial love, forgiveness, prayer, the Eucharist, a just lifestyle, and so on—Christians are already experiencing the Kingdom of God here on Earth. Of course, sin is still a reality, which means that this experience of the Kingdom is only a small taste of the real heaven that awaits us after death.

Church as Sacrament

A sacrament makes visible something real that we cannot see. Jesus Christ is a sacrament because he the visible image of the invisible God. The Church is a sacrament, too. It is a visible sign of a spiritual reality. That reality is the union of people with God and with one another. As a sacrament the Church is also an instrument, or means, of this unity. God works through the Church to accomplish his plan of bringing the whole human race together in communion with him. That is why we call the Church the "sacrament of salvation." When we say that the Church is a sacrament, we recognize that the Church has a visible, earthly aspect and an invisible, spiritual aspect, which is just as real as the visible aspect.

The Holy Spirit, the Church, and Confirmation

We enter the Church, of course, through Baptism. As we will explore more fully in the period of reflection, the power of the Holy Spirit's activity in our life is fully unleashed through Confirmation. But to actively participate in that community of faith, each person must come to a personal recognition of Jesus Christ, become personally aware of Jesus's risen presence and be open to the guidance of the Holy Spirit that Christ shared through his death and Resurrection. The Church is that community of believers who share a most remarkable treasure—the recognition of Christ's presence through the

Holy Spirit and a commitment to the truth of his message about God, whose love is infinite. It is a reality that can truly make one's heart "burn" with joy and peace, (two of the fruits of the Spirit). Faith, hope, and charity (the three theological virtues) dispose us to life in the Trinity where God is known by faith, hoped in and loved for his own sake.

When Jews observe Pentecost, they celebrate the giving of the Law to Moses on Mount Sinai. The Christian feast of Pentecost, however, is a celebration of God's gift of a new kind of law, a law of the Spirit. In the next phase of preparation for Confirmation, the period of reflection, we will explore the significance of what it means to live by the Holy Spirit and continue the mission of Jesus Christ on Earth. You are invited to participate in this exploration and to continue on the journey toward Confirmation and increased participation in the life of the Church.

Looking back, looking ahead

Jot down your thoughts and feelings about the study of Jesus Christ and the Church that has been the focus of this part of your preparation for Confirmation. What is the most important thing you have learned or experienced? Do you have any disappointments or regrets about this part of the process?

What do you hope to learn or gain during the next part of the process? What can you do to help make that possible?

Period of Reflection

As you continue with the process of preparation for Confirmation, you enter into the period of reflection. You began the process with the invitation period, during which you considered your identity as a unique person created in the image of God and reflected on his call to respond to his love with faith. Then, in the period of formation, you carefully considered Jesus Christ—who he was and is, his proclamation of the Kingdom of God, his central teachings, and, of course, his death on the cross and the event that followed it, his Resurrection. You concluded that period by reflecting on Jesus's gift of the Holy Spirit at Pentecost and the mission of the Church in the world.

During the reflection sessions, you will explore what it means to make a commitment to Jesus Christ and his Gospel as a fully initiated member of the Catholic Church. This period begins by focusing on the Holy Spirit, who gives us inspiration, guidance, and strength so that we may live as disciples of Jesus Christ. Then we move on to explore central aspects of the Christian life: prayer, moral living, justice and service, and the celebration of the sacraments. The period of reflection is designed to help you prepare for Confirmation by providing both information and opportunities for prayer and reflection that will shed light on how the Holy Spirit moves in your life and in the Church.

Guided and Strengthened by the Holy Spirit

Every facet of Jesus's life, ministry, and mission was guided, indeed driven, by the Holy Spirit. But who is this Spirit? And what does it mean to be guided by the Holy Spirit? These questions are the focus of this session.

Images of the Holy Spirit

We have never seen the Holy Spirit so we use images to describe and better understand the presence and action of the Spirit in our lives and in the world.

One common image of the Holy Spirit is derived from the meaning of the term *spirit*. The word *spirit* is the English translation of the Hebrew *ruah* and the Greek *pneuma,* which refer to dynamic unseen forces like wind and breath. Wind can be a gentle, refreshing breeze or a powerful gale capable of reshaping everything in its path. Breath means life. Without it we cease to live. When we say the Holy Spirit is like wind or breath, we are saying that the Spirit of God is a dynamic, transforming power and the source of life.

Other images or symbols of the Holy Spirit include water, fire, oil, a cloud, light, a dove, and a hand.

Water signifies the life-giving action of the Spirit in Baptism. Jesus likened the Holy Spirit to rivers of living water that flow out of the hearts of believers (John 7:38).

Fire signifies the power of the Spirit to transform. Just as fire changes whatever it touches, so, too, does the Spirit of the Lord.

The ritual of anointing with oil signifies the gift of Christ's loving presence through the Holy Spirit. The name *Christian* comes from Christ, meaning "the anointed one."

The images of a cloud and light symbolize that the Holy Spirit reveals God the Father's presence (like light) but also hides his full glory (like a cloud). These images appear in scriptural accounts such as Jesus's baptism, the Transfiguration, and Jesus's Ascension.

The dove appears in the Scriptures as a sign of the Father's gift of his Spirit. When Jesus came out of the water after his baptism, the Holy Spirit came

The Spirit whom we experience and celebrate in Confirmation is the same Spirit who was present at the creation of the world.

 Christ has no body now on earth but yours; yours are the only hands with which he can do his work, yours are the only feet with which he can go about the world, yours are the only eyes through which his compassion can shine forth upon a troubled world. Christ has no body on earth now but yours.

—Saint Teresa of Ávila

down upon him in the form of a dove. That is why Christian art often uses a dove to depict the Holy Spirit.

Laying or imposing hands on someone is a sign of the outpouring of the Holy Spirit. The Scriptures recount that Jesus healed and blessed people by laying his hands on them.

The Holy Spirit: Third Person of the Trinity

Each divine person of the Trinity—the Father, Son, and Holy Spirit—is the one God; there is only one Godhead. The Holy Spirit is truly God. Through the grace of the Holy Spirit, faith is kindled in us and the new life that comes from God is communicated to us. Through the Scriptures and Tradition, we know that the Holy Spirit is one of the three persons of the Trinity. Though he was the last of the three persons to be revealed, he has been active in the world since Creation. The Spirit, whom we experience and celebrate in Baptism, the Eucharist, and Confirmation—indeed all the sacraments—is the same Spirit who was present at the creation of the world (see Genesis 1:1–2); the same Spirit who spoke through the prophets of the Old Testament; the same Spirit who came upon Jesus at his baptism (see Luke 3:22) and enabled him to confront and defeat the power of evil during his temptations in the desert (see Luke 4:1–2); the same Spirit of healing love who nourished the sick and hurting at the touch of Jesus; the same Spirit who inspired Jesus to trust in the promises of his Father even as he faced death on the cross; the same Spirit who descended on the Apostles at Pentecost (see Acts of the Apostles 2:2–8); and the same Spirit who has guided the Church toward truth and love over the last two thousand years and enables us to share in the communion of the Holy Trinity. The Holy Spirit will continue to be at work with the Father and the Son until the plan for our salvation is complete.

The Holy Spirit is united with the Father and the Son in an unbreakable bond of love. When the Father sends his Son, he always sends the Spirit. The mission of Jesus Christ and the mission of the Holy Spirit are inseparable, yet their work is distinct. It is Jesus whom we see, a visible image of the invisible God, but it is the Holy Spirit who, while never drawing attention to himself, reveals the Son and the Father. When we pray the Nicene Creed, we confess belief in the Spirit in this way: "We believe in the Holy Spirit, the Lord, the giver of life, *who proceeds from the Father and the Son. With the Father and the Son he is worshiped and glorified. He has spoken through the Prophets* [emphasis added]."

Catechism quote In every liturgical action the Holy Spirit is sent in order to bring us into communion with Christ and so to form his Body. The Holy Spirit is like the sap of the Father's vine which bears fruit on its branches. The most intimate cooperation of the Holy Spirit and the Church is achieved in the liturgy. The Spirit, who is the Spirit of communion, abides indefectibly in the Church. For this reason the Church is the great sacrament of divine communion which gathers God's scattered children together. Communion with the Holy Trinity and fraternal communion are inseparably the fruit of the Spirit in the liturgy.

—*Catechism*, no. 1108

Belief in the Holy Spirit also means believing that the Son of God is present and active in our lives today. When we feel the power of God's forgiveness, sense that he is asking us to do something, speak of his action in our lives today, or see him at work in the lives of other people, it is by the power of the Holy Spirit. We are also talking about the presence of the Spirit of God when we speak of the Father giving us gifts or charisms. "Now there are varieties of gifts, but the same Spirit; and there are varieties of services, but the same Lord; and there are varieties of activities, but it is the same God who activates all of them in everyone. To each is given the manifestation of the Spirit for the common good" (1 Corinthians 12:4–7). The Holy Spirit has given each of us gifts and a corresponding challenge, that is, to use them for the sake of others and to build up the Church, the Body of Christ.

The presence of the Holy Spirit is an amazing gift and a great source of hope for us. Through the Spirit we come to know God's love and open ourselves to its transforming power. The Holy Spirit gives us the assurance that Christ, the Son of God, is always with us.

Prayer to the Holy Spirit

Leader: Come, Holy Spirit, fill the hearts of your faithful;

Response: Enkindle in them the fire of your love.

Leader: Send forth your Spirit, and they will be created.

Response: And you will renew the face of the earth.

Leader: Let us pray: Lord, by the light of the Holy Spirit, you have taught the hearts of the faithful. In the same Spirit, help us to relish what is right and always rejoice in your consolation. We ask this through Christ our Lord.

Response: Amen.

The Holy Spirit in Liturgy

When we celebrate sacraments, we call on the Holy Spirit to be present in our midst. Another word for this special kind of call is *epiclesis,* which is Greek for "invocation." The celebrant, praying on behalf of all the people who are gathered, begs the Father to send the Spirit. Here are some examples from the sacraments of initiation:

Baptism. When blessing the water the celebrant touches it and prays, "We ask you, Father, with your Son to send the Holy Spirit upon the water of this font. May all who are buried with Christ in the death of baptism rise also with him to newness of life" (Rite of Baptism).

The Eucharist. During the Eucharistic Prayer II, the celebrant prays, "Let your Spirit come upon these gifts to make them holy, so that they may become for us the body and blood of our Lord, Jesus Christ." Later, during the same prayer, he invokes the Spirit again in this prayer for unity: "May all of us who share in the body and blood of Christ be brought together in unity by the Holy Spirit" (*Sacramentary,* pages 549 and 550).

Confirmation. The bishop prays for the candidates, saying to God the Father, "Send your Holy Spirit upon them to be their Helper and Guide" (*Rite of Confirmation,* number 25).

Our sacramental prayers of invocation share a common theme. We pray not only that the Holy Spirit will be present and change things, such as the bread and wine in the Eucharist, but that the Spirit of God will change us and bring us into greater communion with him and one another so that we might be the Body of Christ in the world.

Bible byte

A shoot shall come out from
    the stump of Jesse,
and a branch shall
    grow out of his roots.
The spirit of the Lord shall rest
    on him,
    the spirit of wisdom and
    understanding,
    the spirit of counsel and might,
    the spirit of knowledge and
    the fear of the Lord.
His delight shall be in the fear of
    the Lord.

—Isaiah 11:1–3

Born of the Spirit

In talking to Nicodemus about the necessity of being born of the Spirit, Jesus said, "The wind blows where it chooses, and you hear the sound of it, but you do not know where it comes from or where it goes. So it is with everyone who is born of the Spirit" (John 3:8). Think about ways we encounter wind: gentle breezes that bring coolness, steady winds and gusts that make sailboats move and generate power, violent winds that are capable of reshaping the earth. We cannot see the wind, only its effects. Write about how the Holy Spirit's action in your life can be likened to the power and movement of wind?

Prayer: Communion with God

Our focus in this session is the Catholic practice without which none of the other elements of a Christian life is possible—the practice of prayer. It is so important because through prayer, the Holy Spirit unites us to Jesus Christ and transforms our hearts. Every session in this program has included one or more experiences of group or communal prayer. But here our concern is the kind of prayer we must practice in our personal life if we hope to grow in our experience of and relationship with God.

Many definitions of prayer exist, including "talking with God" or "lifting one's mind and heart to God" or "communicating with God in a relationship of love."

Communication certainly includes talking and listening. But when people in love with each other or in deep friendship with each other communicate, they do so in a variety of ways:

> They talk and listen to each other with words. They engage in verbal communication in many ways—most often with short comments and asides by telling stories, or by carrying on extended, deep conversations.

> They communicate in nonverbal ways too, which is often more effective than verbal communication. They spend time with each other and do things together. They turn to each other for support and comfort when in need or in pain, sometimes just by holding each other. At times they may just sit in silence, or together look at the same sight in wonder and awe. All these are forms of communication in a genuine relationship of love.

There are parallel experiences for all these forms of communication in a love relationship with God, and each one reflects a different kind of personal prayer. In this session we explore just a few of the many kinds of personal prayer.

Forms of Prayer

God wants to be in relationship with you in every aspect of your life—in all your concerns, gifts, faults, and feelings. This gives rise to different forms of prayer—adoration, contrition, petition, intercession, thanksgiving, and praise—that connect to different times and situations in your life.

Bible byte [Jesus said], "Ask, and it will be given you; search, and you will find; knock, and the door will be opened for you. . . . Is there anyone among you who, if your child asks for a fish, will give a snake instead of a fish? Or if the child asks for an egg, will give a scorpion? If you then, who are evil, know how to give good gifts to your children, how much more will the heavenly Father give the Holy Spirit to those who ask him!"

—Luke 11:9–13

Catechism quote The Holy Spirit, whose anointing permeates our whole being, is the interior Master of Christian prayer. . . . To be sure, there are as many paths of prayer as there are persons who pray, but it is the same Spirit acting in all and with all.

—*Catechism*, no. 2672

Adoration. The first commandment says we acknowledge God alone as Creator and Savior and worship him alone as the source of all blessings in our lives. Prayers of adoration confirm our commitment to God's primacy in our lives.

Contrition. When we are contrite, we are apologetic. Prayers of contrition are our quiet moments with God to express our sorrow for anything that may have taken us away from him.

Petition. To petition is to make a request. We ask God for something we need. When we pray in this manner, we express an awareness of our relationship with God and our absolute need for him.

Intercession. This is a type of petitionary prayer that focuses on other people instead of ourselves. We ask God for something for someone else. We pray for friends and loved ones as well as enemies. We also pray for people we don't know, especially those in need of food, shelter, and companionship and all who are suffering.

Thanksgiving. This is a prayer of gratitude for all that God has given us. Saint Paul emphasized its importance: "Give thanks in all circumstances; for this is the will of God in Christ Jesus for you" (1 Thessalonians 5:18). Our most full expression of thanksgiving occurs in the celebration of the Eucharist.

Praise. A prayer of praise is a joyful expression inspired by our love for God. Our focus, however, is not on something God has done for us. Rather, we praise and extol God simply because HE IS. We can praise in song, in dance, in word, and in actions.

Christian Meditation

One prayer form that is particularly helpful is called meditation. Meditation engages our thoughts, emotions, imagination, and desires in seeking a deeper union with God. There are many different methods for Christian meditation. One basic method involves these steps:

> **Pick the right time and place.** Choose a regular time to pray when you are normally alert and able to focus. Look for a place where you know you won't be disturbed during your time of prayer.

> **Prepare to pray by relaxing your body.** Use techniques like "tense and relax" muscle exercises and deep breathing to relax your body so that you can devote your attention to prayer.

> **Choose a word or phrase to focus your attention on God.** Some people like to use one word only, perhaps a favorite name for

God (like Abba), or the name *Jesus.* Others use a short phrase such as "Come, Holy Spirit."

› **Connect the sacred words with your breathing.** Silently repeat your chosen word or phrase in time with your breathing. The intent is to use the repetition as an aid to focusing on and remaining open to the presence of God. For example, you might say, "Jesus, my friend," with each inhalation and "be with me now," with each exhalation. If you become distracted, simply focus again on repeating your word or phrase.

Experiment with this method of meditation. You may find that those few minutes every day make a lifetime of difference in your relationship with God.

What Is Prayer?

Prayer is a relationship. It is God's action through the Holy Spirit and it is our response. Here's how the American edition of the *Catechism* defines *prayer* in its glossary:

> [Prayer is] the elevation of the mind and heart to God in praise of his glory; a petition made to God for some desired good, or in thanksgiving for a good received, or in intercession for others before God. Through prayer the Christian experiences a communion with God through Christ in the Church. (Page 894)

The Holy Spirit teaches us how to pray and is like living water that wells up within us when we pray. The "Spirit is offered us at all times, in the events of each day, to make prayer spring up from us" (*Catechism,* number 2659).

Setting a TRAP for God

One very ancient and helpful evening prayer is called an *examen,* which is related to the term *examination.* But this is a much less scary exercise than the word *examination* might normally suggest!

In Jesus's time people set traps to catch animals for food. The trappers had to be alert and focused in order to catch their prey, just as a pray-er must be prepared to grasp God's message. The TRAP acronym stands for these four steps in the *examen:*

Thank: Thank God for all the good things that happened during the day, trying to name those as clearly as possible.

Review: Reflect on your attitude and actions during the day. Try to be very honest in assessing both the good as well as the bad or destructive things you did or said or felt.

Ask: For any actions or attitudes that hurt others or kept you from being the person God calls you to be, ask God to forgive you and help you to make amends. Or, ask God to give you what you need, such as guidance when you are facing difficult decisions or challenges.

Promise to change: Make a commitment, with the grace of God, to do better tomorrow.

The regular practice of the evening *examen* is a powerful tool for growing as a disciple of Jesus.

> (This section is adapted from Delgatto and Shrader, *Catechetical Sessions on Christian Prayer,* page 64.)

Work as if everything depends on you. Pray as if everything depends on God.

—Saint Ignatius of Loyola

The Lord's Prayer

The disciples said to Jesus, "Lord, teach us to pray" (Luke 11:1). In response, he taught them the Lord's Prayer. This prayer, which is a summary of the Gospel, gets its name because it comes to us from Jesus. The traditional form that we pray in our liturgies is drawn from the Gospel of Matthew (6:9–13):

> Our Father in heaven,
>> hallowed be your name.
>> Your kingdom come.
>> Your will be done,
>>> on earth as it is in heaven.
>> Give us this day our daily bread.
>> And forgive us our debts,
>>> as we also have forgiven our debtors.
>> And do not bring us to the time of trial,
>>> but rescue us from the evil one.

After we invoke God by saying "Our Father in heaven," we pray seven petitions. The first three focus on the Father, the one whom we love. We make no mention of ourselves. We pray "hallowed be your name, your kingdom come, your will be done." The final four express our desires. We ask, in the fourth and fifth petitions, that the Father nourish us and free us from sin. In the last two, we pray that he will help us be victorious in the struggle of good over evil. When we pray the words of the Lord's Prayer, the Holy Spirit gives them life in our hearts.

Prayer from morning to night

Try to develop a pattern of regular prayer that sets a kind of rhythm for your day. Morning and evening prayer ought to become a personal habit. And it's helpful to have a method of prayer that we can rely on anytime, anywhere.

With the direction of your leader, thoughtfully complete the sentence starters below to help develop a regular pattern of personal prayer that works for you:

My preferred morning prayer is . . .

My chosen anytime, anywhere prayer is . . .

My preferred evening prayer is . . .

Christian Morality:
What Does Love Look Like?

Jesus called us to an ideal love when he said, "As the Father has loved me, so I have loved you; abide in my love" (John 15:9). He made his instructions a little clearer when he said, "This is my commandment, that you love one another as I have loved you" (15:12). That statement is the foundation of Christian morality.

The Scriptures tell us a lot about what real love looks like. Love is the highest law—love directed to God, to neighbor, to self, and to all creation. When a Pharisee asked Jesus to tell him which commandment of the Jewish Law was the greatest, Jesus summed up the Ten Commandments in two statements: "The first is, '. . . You shall love the Lord your God with all your heart, and with all your soul, and with all your mind, and with all your strength.' The second is this, 'You shall love your neighbor as yourself.' There is no other commandment greater than these" (Mark 12:29–31). The Reign of God is love. Recall our earlier discussion of the Reign of God during the formation period: The Reign, or Kingdom, of God is the rule of God's love over the hearts of people and a new social order based on unconditional love of God and others. Love means being deeply concerned about the dignity and welfare of other people. It means respecting all life because we are in relationship with all life. This is central to Christian life.

Rules for Love: The Ten Commandments

God has revealed some rules for living a life of love that reflects his Kingdom. At Mount Sinai God promised to make the Israelites his own people, protecting and caring for them. In exchange the Israelites had to keep the Law, a large body of rules given by God to help the people survive as a community and live in right relationship with one another and with God. This was known as the Sinai Covenant. The cornerstone of the Covenant was the Ten Commandments.

Today the Ten Commandments continue to be fundamental moral precepts. Yet they are the minimum requirements for a life of love. Jesus told his followers not to disregard or forget these commandments, but to go beyond them to fulfill the great commandment of love.

The following is the traditional catechetical formula of the Ten Commandments from the *Catechism* (pages 496–497):

1. I am the LORD, your God: you shall not have strange gods before me.

2. You shall not take the name of the LORD your God in vain.

3. Remember to keep holy the LORD's Day.

4. Honor your father and your mother.

5. You shall not kill.

6. You shall not commit adultery.

7. You shall not steal.

8. You shall not bear false witness against your neighbor.

9. You shall not covet your neighbor's wife.

10. You shall not covet your neighbor's goods.

It's Only Natural

When we listen to the message of Creation and to the voice of conscience, every person can come to certainty about the existence of God. This means that the foundational moral orientation of every person toward the moral good is, in a sense, built into our very being. God's law is present in the heart of each person. We call this natural law.

Saint Thomas Aquinas, a thirteenth-century Italian priest commonly accepted as one of the greatest theologians in the history of the Church, put it this way:

> The natural law is nothing other than the light of understanding placed in us by God; through it we know what we must do and what we must avoid. God has given this light or law at the creation.[10] (Quoted in *Catechism,* number 1955)

Living the Moral Life

When we deliberately fail to follow God's command to love others, we commit sin. As we discussed during the formation period, sins are the things we deliberately think, say, do, or fail to do contrary to the eternal law of God.

Catechism quote

True happiness is not found in riches or well-being, in human fame or power, or in any human achievement—however beneficial it may be—such as science, technology, and art, or indeed in any creature, but in God alone, the source of every good and of all love.

—*Catechism,* no. 1723

They offend God and defy reason. All of us sin, but we are obliged to follow the moral law, which urges us "to do what is good and avoid what is evil" (*Catechism,* number 1713). The Holy Spirit inspires and moves us, turning us toward God and away from sin. This grace, which we receive through Baptism, is something that we have not earned. It is pure, undeserved gift given in love that enables us to accept forgiveness and live in closer relationship with God.

Because of sin, it is not easy for us to do what is good and loving. One thing we can do to make it easier is to put some effort into developing good habits that help us avoid sin and choose the good. We call these habits virtues. Four virtues, called cardinal virtues, play a pivotal role in Christian life because all the other virtues flow from them. With God's help we can acquire and practice these virtues and lead the kind of moral life that brings us into closer communion with God.

The four cardinal virtues are prudence, justice, fortitude, and temperance. Prudence is the habit of thinking before acting. The prudent person uses reason to figure out the true good in every situation and then to choose the right way to achieve it. Justice is the virtue of giving to God and to our neighbors what they are due. The just person thinks about the needs of other people, recognizes their God-given dignity, and reaches out to them with love. Fortitude is the strength to live morally even in difficult situations. A person with fortitude is able to resist temptations and make sacrifices in order to do good. Temperance is the self-control that keeps one's appetite for pleasure from becoming extreme. It doesn't mean we can't have fun. The temperate person develops the habit of setting limits, however, because too much of a good thing can get in the way of the moral life and separate us from God.

Sometimes we truly desire to do what is right, but we have trouble assessing the options before us. Due to the complexity of life and some of the situations we face in our relationships, it is not always easy to know which choices are the moral ones. It is important to keep in mind that it is a mistake to base your evaluation of the morality of human actions solely on intention or circumstances (peer pressure, duress, environment, outcome, and so on). This is because some actions are always wrong. In those cases it doesn't matter whether something good results or an individual's intentions are good. Some examples of actions that are always immoral are blasphemy (insulting or showing contempt for God), murder, perjury, and adultery.

The Desire for Happiness

Everyone wants to be happy. It is part of being human. God has placed this desire in our hearts in order to draw us to himself, the one who alone can fulfill this desire. The goal of human life is to become like God and achieve the ultimate bliss of eternal life. The Church uses the word *beatitude* to refer to this state of sheer joy and happiness.

The Beatitudes "respond to the desire for happiness that God has placed in the human heart" (see Matthew 5:3–12 and Luke 6:20–26) (*Catechism*, number 1725). He describes Beatitude people with statements like, "Blessed are the poor in spirit, for theirs is the kingdom of heaven" and "Blessed are those who hunger and thirst for righteousness, for they will be filled." These statements are at the heart of Jesus's message. They give us hope and help us to understand that God—not wealth, achievement, or popularity—is the source of true happiness. The Beatitudes guide us by giving us insight into the actions and attitudes that characterize Christian life and challenge us to make moral choices about earthly goods so that we may learn to love God above all things, and so that one day, by the grace of the Holy Spirit, we may enter into the joy of divine life.

Our Final Destiny

Catholic Connection If death is not the end of life but a new beginning, what finally becomes of us? Here are the basic Catholic teachings about the "last things":

> ➤ Every human being at the time of death faces God as the person she or he has finally become. The person's heart and actions are judged by Jesus Christ in what is called the particular judgment and she or he receives either reward or punishment.

> ➤ If the person has been closed to a relationship with God during life and has chosen in freedom to turn away from God's love, she or he will lose the perfect happiness for which human beings were created. Catholic Tradition calls the reality of eternal separation from God hell.

> ➤ If the person throughout life chose to be open to and responsive to God's love, then at death that person will be united with God and enjoy perfect happiness eternally. This is heaven, and we cannot possibly imagine how wonderful it will be (see 1 Corinthians 2:9).

Bible byte **Psalm 1**

They are happy who,
    putting all their trust in the cross,
        have plunged into the water
of life (from an author of the second century). (Copyright © ICEL)

Happy indeed is the man
    who follows not the counsel
        of the wicked;
nor lingers in the way of sinners
nor sits in the company of scorners,
but whose delight is the
    law of the Lord
and who ponders his law
    day and night.

He is like a tree that is planted
    beside the flowing waters,
that yields its fruit in due season
    and whose leaves shall
        never fade;
and all that he does shall prosper.
Not so are the wicked, not so!

For they like winnowed chaff
    shall be driven away by the wind.
When the wicked are judged they
    shall not stand,
nor find room among those
    who are just;
for the Lord guards the way
    of the just
but the way of the wicked
    leads to doom.

Heart link I never look at the masses
          as my responsibility.
I look at the individual.
I can love only one person at a time.
I can feed only one person at a time.
     Just one, one, one.
You get closer to Christ by coming closer
     to each other. As Jesus said,
          "Whatever you do to the least of
     my brethren, you do to me."
So you begin . . . I begin.
     I picked up one person—
maybe if I didn't pick up that one person
I wouldn't have picked up 42,000.
     The whole work is only a drop in the
ocean. But if I didn't put the drop in,
     the ocean would be one drop less.
Same thing for you
     same thing in your family
          same thing in the church
               where you go
     just begin . . . one, one, one.

—Mother Teresa

> Very importantly, we are not "sent" to heaven or hell by God, but we "arrive" in heaven or hell as a consequence of how we live our life.

> To those who die in God's grace and friendship yet continue to carry obstacles to total union with God, he offers such people an opportunity for purification, and we call that purgatory. When we pray for these people, we can help them achieve total union with God in heaven.

> Human beings cannot earn their way into heaven. Everything we have received is a gift from God. It is because of God's initiative that people receive the initial grace of conversion. Only because of this gift and the help of the Holy Spirit are individuals able to merit for themselves and others the grace needed to attain eternal life.

> Faith, our free response to God's initiative, is necessary for salvation.

> At the end of the world, on "the last day," all the dead will be raised. Jesus Christ will come again and will judge everyone. "In the presence of Christ, who is Truth itself, the truth of each man's relationship with God will be laid bare[11]" (*Catechism,* number 1039). This final judgment is called the general judgment or last judgment. Because our concept of time is likely to be meaningless after death, it is not possible to understand exactly how the particular judgment and the last judgment relate to each other.

> At the end of time, God's justice and love will reign and his plan for creation will be fulfilled. "We shall know the ultimate meaning of the whole work of creation and of the entire economy of salvation and understand the marvellous ways by which his Providence led everything towards its final end" (*Catechism,* number 1040).

Jesus shows us what love looks like

Write here the Gospel citation assigned by your leader.

What is the primary teaching of Jesus reflected in this passage?

Name three ways that teaching might apply to the world of young people today.

Counting the costs of love

Jesus's command to those who wish to be his disciples can sound nearly overwhelming: "Love one another as I have loved you." How do you feel when confronted by Jesus's command to love? Looking at your life right now as honestly as you can, what does love call you to do or to change? Are you willing to do it?

Christian Service: Witnessing to God's Justice

At the beginning of his ministry, according to the Gospel of Luke, Jesus went to the synagogue on the Sabbath day, stood up in the midst of the people, and read the following passage from the prophet Isaiah:

> "The Spirit of the Lord is upon me,
> because he has anointed me
> to bring good news to the poor.
> He has sent me to proclaim release to the captives
> and recovery of sight to the blind,
> to let the oppressed go free,
> to proclaim the year of the Lord's favor."
>
> (Luke 4:18–19)

After he finished reading, he sat down. The eyes of all the people were fixed on him, and he said to them, "Today this scripture has been fulfilled in your hearing" (see Luke 4:16–21). Jesus's choice of Scripture and his words following the reading announce that he is the anointed one who will bring justice to the world.

We understand our mission as members of the Church in relationship to Jesus's mission. To live faithfully in the Holy Spirit and continue Jesus's mission on Earth, we all must cooperate in God's work of bringing about a more just society through service to others, especially poor and vulnerable people. Justice prevails in society when we respect the God-given dignity of all people and we are able to live in loving relationships with God and one another.

The Gospel of Matthew expresses this challenging dimension of Christian life in a story about the last judgment:

> When the Son of Man comes in his glory, . . . he will separate people one from another as a shepherd separates the sheep from the goats, and he will put the sheep at his right hand and the goats at the left. Then the king will say to those at his right hand, "Come, you that are blessed by my Father, inherit the kingdom prepared for you from the foundation of the world; for I was hungry and you gave me food, I was thirsty and you gave me something to drink, I was a stranger and you welcomed me, I was naked and you gave me clothing, I was sick and you took care of me, I was in prison and you visited me." Then the righteous will answer him, "Lord, when was it that we saw you hungry and gave you food, or thirsty and

 We believe that every person is precious, that people are more important than things, and that the measure of every institution is whether it threatens or enhances the life and dignity of the human person.

—*Sharing Catholic Social Teaching*, page 4

gave you something to drink? And when was it that we saw you a stranger and welcomed you, or naked and gave you clothing? And when was it that we saw you sick or in prison and visited you?" And the king will answer them, "Truly I tell you, just as you did it to one of the least of these who are members of my family, you did it to me." (25:31–40)

Catechism quote Sins give rise to social situations and institutions that are contrary to the divine goodness. "Structures of sin" are the expression and effect of personal sins. They lead their victims to do evil in their turn. In an analogous sense, they constitute a "social sin."[12]

—*Catechism,* no. 1869

The Two Feet of Christian Justice

Understanding that the Gospels challenge us to work for justice is easy. Figuring out exactly what we ought to be doing in our day-to-day lives, and then doing it, is more difficult. Mother Teresa's advice in the Heart Link quote—begin by focusing on one person at a time—is wise. It is also helpful to distinguish between two different types of service—direct action and social action—and to recognize that both are necessary in the work against injustice.

Direct actions are the things we do to address the immediate needs of another person. Working at a soup kitchen, organizing a canned-food drive, buying Christmas gifts for poor families, and donating clothing are examples of this type of service.

Social actions are the things we do to eliminate the causes of injustice. This type of work for justice is aimed at changing some aspect of society—its laws or policies regarding such things as affordable housing, labor, literacy, racial equality, or the environment—so that individuals will be able to live the full, dignified lives that God intends for all of us. Effective social action involves analyzing unjust situations to determine the causes of the injustice and to identify the best ways to respond.

A person's work for justice often begins with direct action because it involves clear, concrete steps that help people directly. The work of trying to meet the immediate needs of poor and suffering people is very important. But it can be frustrating if the underlying causes of the injustices people suffer remain unchanged. We must ask why injustices persist and figure out ways to create change. Direct action and social action are sometimes called the two feet of Christian justice because progress toward a more just society is dependent on people carrying out both types of service.

The call to work for justice can be overwhelming. Human sin contributes to misery and injustice throughout the world. It can be helpful to remember that God does not expect us to transform the world by ourselves. Ultimately, at the end of time, God will bring about justice and peace for all when he fully realizes his Kingdom. Our responsibility as members of the Body of Christ is to cooperate with God's plan and allow the Holy Spirit to work through us so that the world can become a more loving place.

Christian Service

Catholic Social Teaching

Catholic Connection The Catholic Church has a long tradition of advocating justice. "Catholic social teaching" refers to a series of official Church documents that examines social situations in light of the Scriptures and Tradition and provides guidelines for action. The U.S. Catholic bishops, in *Sharing Catholic Social Teaching,* identify seven major themes that summarize the Church's social teaching:

1. **Life and Dignity of the Human Person.** Human life is sacred and . . . . the dignity of the human person is the foundation of a moral vision for society.

2. **Call to Family, Community, and Participation.** People have a right and a duty to participate in society, seeking together the common good and well-being of all, especially the poor and vulnerable.

3. **Rights and Responsibilities.** Every person has a fundamental right to life and a right to those things required for human decency. Corresponding to these rights are duties and responsibilities—to one another, to our families, and to the larger society.

4. **Option for the Poor and Vulnerable.** A basic moral test is how our most vulnerable members are faring. In a society marred by deepening divisions between rich and poor, our tradition recalls the story of the Last Judgment (Matthew 25:31–46) and instructs us to put the needs of the poor and vulnerable first.

5. **The Dignity of Work and the Rights of Workers.** Work is more than a way to make a living; it is a form of continuing participation in God's creation. If the dignity of work is to be protected, then the basic rights of workers must be respected—the right to productive work, to decent and fair wages, to organize and join unions, to private property, and to economic initiative.

6. **Solidarity.** We are our brothers' and sisters' keepers, wherever they live. We are one human family, whatever our national, racial, ethnic, economic, and ideological differences. Learning to practice the virtue of solidarity means learning that "loving our neighbor" has global dimensions in an interdependent world.

7. **Care for God's Creation.** Care for the earth is not just an Earth Day slogan, it is a requirement of our faith. We are called to protect people and the planet, living our faith in relationship with all of God's creation.

 Bible bytes Be doers of the word, and not merely hearers.

—James 1:22

What good is it, my brothers and sisters, if you say you have faith but do not have works? Can faith save you? If a brother or sister is naked and lacks daily food, and one of you says to them, "Go in peace; keep warm and eat your fill," and yet you do not supply their bodily needs, what is the good of that? So faith by itself, if it has no works, is dead.

—James 2:14–17

(Pages 4–6)

Action for justice

Identify an unjust situation affecting someone in your community. What direct actions would help this person?

Reflect on the underlying causes of the situation. Try to identify some social actions that would help to eliminate one or more of the causes.

Sacraments of Initiation

As the date of your Confirmation draws nearer, we now move directly into a more detailed discussion of the sacramental life of the Church. This session will explore the way the early Church celebrated the sacraments of initiation and will help you understand the meaning and significance of what we do today when we celebrate the sacraments.

Baptism in the Early Church

Baptism in the early Church was a powerful and moving experience. The ritual utilized rich symbols and actions that conveyed deep meaning to those who participated. Imagine walking down three steps into the waters of the baptismal pool, being immersed three times by the bishop, and then coming out of the water a new creation.

Baptism in the first few centuries of the Church's history was celebrated primarily with adults. Baptism of infant members of Christian families, however, gradually became normal practice and is still most common today.

In the early Church, a person preparing for Baptism was called a *catechumen*. This word comes from a Greek term related to sound and hearing. A catechumen is one who hears Jesus's Good News proclaimed by the Church. The preparation period was called the catechumenate. Lasting about three years, the catechumenate was a time for praying, fasting, studying, and being of service to others. During this time the catechumen listened to the word of God and explored the Christian way of life. (In your process of preparation, the period of formation parallels the catechumenate in the early Church.)

The final intense stage of preparation for baptism in the early Church lasted forty days and evolved into what we know as Lent. (In your preparation the period of reflection is intended to parallel this part of the early Church's practice.) Baptism, the final step in the original process, took place during the Easter Vigil—the evening before the Easter celebration of the Resurrection. In the early Church, the Easter Vigil was the only time when baptisms were performed. Even after the actual ceremony, further study was expected and more knowledge about the Christian "mysteries" was provided to the newly initiated members. (The period of mission in your preparation process parallels this part of the early Church's approach to the sacraments of initiation.)

Bible byte

As God's chosen ones, holy and beloved, clothe yourselves with compassion, kindness, humility, meekness, and patience. Bear with one another and, if anyone has a complaint against another, forgive each other; just as the Lord has forgiven you, so you also must forgive. Above all, clothe yourselves with love, which binds everything together in perfect harmony. And let the peace of Christ rule in your hearts, to which indeed you were called in the one body. And be thankful. Let the word of Christ dwell in you richly; teach and admonish one another in all wisdom; and with gratitude in your hearts sing psalms, hymns, and spiritual songs to God. And whatever you do, in word or deed, do everything in the name of the Lord Jesus, giving thanks to God the Father through him.

—Colossians 3:12–17

Baptism at the Easter Vigil

The Easter Vigil ceremony was preceded by ritual bathing on Holy Thursday and by two days of fasting. On the Saturday night of the vigil, all the catechumens gathered, men in one room and women in another. Their sponsors—the persons who had guided them toward their new birth—were there. They were called fathers and mothers by the catechumens because they performed a parental role. Later, sponsors would become known as godparents.

At the start of the Easter Vigil ceremony, the catechumens faced the west, the place of sunset and darkness. They stretched out their arms and denounced Satan. Then suddenly they turned to the east and shouted their commitment to Christ. This physical turnabout by the catechumens marked their spiritual turnabout, or conversion. The East was considered the place of light, of the rising sun, and of new life. (Throughout the Middle Ages, churches were built facing the east.)

Next, the catechumens went to a room with a pool that was often modeled after the Roman public baths. They stripped off their old clothing, had oil poured over their body, and stepped down into the waist-deep waters. The bishop submerged the catechumens in the water, usually three times—in the name of the Father, the Son, and the Holy Spirit. The catechumens then emerged from the other side of the pool and received new white robes. The bishop anointed them, again with oil, and embraced them in a sign of peace and welcome.

Finally, the catechumens were led into the room where the Eucharist was celebrated. For the first time, on Easter Sunday, they participated in the total Eucharistic celebration. Prior to baptism the catechumens attended Mass only until the end of the homily. As a matter of fact, the first part of the Mass was called the Mass of the Catechumens because the prayers, readings, and homily were intended to give instruction to the catechumens. What a joy it must have been for the newly baptized, after three years of preparation, to share the Eucharist with their friends and family for the first time! And what a joy for the rest of the community to welcome these long-awaited newcomers to their special Easter meal!

The process of preparing for initiation at the Easter Vigil demanded a great deal of time and dedication from those who wanted to become members of the Church. Remember, though, that just prior to this time, the Church had

 You have followed God's light and the way of the Gospel now lies open to you. . . . Walk in the light of Christ and learn to trust in his wisdom.

—From the RCIA rite of acceptance

been an illegal, persecuted group. Accepting a candidate presented a grave risk to the whole community.

At the same time, the leaders realized that baptism was meant to be a sustained joy, not just a moment of excitement. Developing a joyful, loving community demanded a profound initiation. In recent years the Church has revised the adult Rite of Christian Initiation to recapture the sacrifice, spirit, and joy of the ritual in the early Church.

Three Sacraments of Initiation

Originally Baptism, Confirmation, and the Eucharist were combined in one initiation ritual. Later on, so many candidates sought initiation into the Church that the bishops had difficulty presiding at all the rituals. Yet it was considered essential that the bishops conduct them.

To handle the increased numbers of converts, the Eastern Church decided to allow their priests to baptize, confirm, and celebrate the Eucharist with the initiates. In the East, Confirmation is administered immediately after Baptism and is followed by participation in the Eucharist; this tradition highlights the unity of the three sacraments of Christian Initiation. In the West, the priests baptized initiates but delayed the rest of the ceremony until the bishop was available to "confirm" the initiation. Eventually in the Western Church, the baptized members began to participate in the Eucharist before Confirmation. Until recently, the sacraments of initiation remained separate and were celebrated in the sequence of Baptism, the Eucharist, and Confirmation

You have been enlightened by Christ. Walk always as children of the light and keep the flame of faith alive in your hearts.

—From the RCIA celebration of the sacraments of initiation

The Seven Sacraments

The seven sacraments of the Church are the means by which we share in the new life offered by Christ through the gift of the Holy Spirit. They are the actions of the Spirit at work in the Church and symbolize the life and work of Jesus Christ. They build up the Body of Christ and they nourish, strengthen, and express the faith of individuals. The sacraments help us remember, celebrate, and participate in the Paschal mystery. That is, through them we remember the life, ministry, and death of Jesus, and celebrate anew his risen presence among us. The sacraments do this in the following ways:

> The three sacraments of initiation together—Baptism, Confirmation, and the Eucharist—initiate new members and help

the community of faith remember Jesus Christ and celebrate his risen presence within the Church today. In Baptism the waters of rebirth are signs of death and life: the baptized person symbolically dies to all that is sinful and then lives in Christ. In Confirmation the anointing with chrism and the words of Confirmation symbolize and impart the fullness of the Holy Spirit to the baptized person. In the Eucharist we share in the body and blood of Christ and commit to living out the death and Resurrection of Christ in our daily lives.

> The sacraments of Penance and Reconciliation and the Anointing of the Sick are sacraments of healing. Penance centers on spiritual healing; God's forgiveness of the sinner is celebrated in the words of the sacrament. In the Anointing of the Sick, the Church anoints and prays for and with those whose physical sickness has made it impossible or difficult for them to be active in the community.

> In the sacraments at the service of communion—Holy Orders and Matrimony—the Church celebrates its ministry to all people. In the sacrament of Holy Orders—through prayer, the laying on of hands, and anointing—men are ordained to serve the Church as bishops, priests, or deacons. Matrimony celebrates the love between a man and a woman, as well as their vow to serve each other and to reflect to the whole Church the love of God for all humankind. Marriage is a covenant of faithful and fruitful love that reflects the union of Christ and the Church.

The Nicene Creed

A creed (based on the Latin word *credo,* meaning "I believe") is a formal statement of the beliefs of the Church. In the ancient rite of Baptism, the presider would engage the candidates in a question-and-answer dialogue about their beliefs. We use this interrogatory type of creedal expression in liturgy today when we make and renew our baptismal promises, which you will be invited to do at your Confirmation.

Declaratory creeds were also used early in the Church's history. These were composed of statements. At Sunday Mass today, Catholics join together to profess their beliefs using a declaratory creed commonly known as the Nicene Creed. Often referred to as the profession of faith, the Nicene Creed was written over sixteen hundred years ago. It is held in common by Roman

Catholics, Eastern Rite Catholics, Anglicans, Episcopalians, and all major Protestant denominations.

In light of all you have learned in the process of preparation for Confirmation, try to reflect on the words of the creed in a thoughtful and prayerful way as you share it with your fellow candidates and, in the future, with countless other believers. "To say the Credo with faith is to enter into communion with God, Father, Son, and Holy Spirit, and also with the whole Church which transmits the faith to us and in whose midst we believe" (*Catechism,* number 197).

The Nicene Creed

We believe in one God, the Father, the Almighty, maker of heaven and earth, of all that is, seen and unseen.

We believe in one Lord, Jesus Christ, the only Son of God eternally begotten of the Father, God from God, Light from Light, true God from true God, begotten, not made, one in Being with the Father. Through him all things were made.

For us men and for our salvation, he came down from heaven: by the power of the Holy Spirit he was born of the Virgin Mary, and became man. For our sake he was crucified under Pontius Pilate; he suffered, died, and was buried. On the third day he rose again in fulfillment of the Scriptures; he ascended into heaven and is seated at the right hand of the Father. He will come again in glory to judge the living and the dead, and his kingdom will have no end.

We believe in the Holy Spirit, the Lord, the giver of life, who proceeds from the Father and the Son. With the Father and the Son he is worshiped and glorified. He has spoken through the Prophets.

We believe in one holy catholic and apostolic Church. We acknowledge one baptism for the forgiveness of sins. We look for the resurrection of the dead, and the life of the world to come.

Amen.

Confirming a deeper bond with the Church

Recall the feelings you experienced during the opening exercise of this session, as well as the thoughts and feelings you have when you think ahead to the celebration of Confirmation. What does being Catholic now mean to you? Are you ready to more fully embrace—and be embraced by—the Catholic community of faith?

Baptism: Born in the Holy Spirit

You likely began your journey as a Catholic when you were baptized as an infant. During this session we will recall that wondrous event, especially the powerful symbol of water that is so central to this sacrament. The session also invites you to see and to celebrate the relationship between Baptism and Confirmation. At one level, Confirmation is an invitation to embrace more fully and consciously the baptism that was offered you as a gift so many years ago.

Water: Symbol of Life and Death

Think about your experiences with water for a moment. What comes to mind? Bathing, drinking a cool glass of refreshing water, fun times swimming or boating, a good soaking rain that is so important for nourishing the earth? Perhaps you are thinking about some things that are less positive: flooding, destruction caused by a powerful rainstorm, a scary experience of getting caught in a strong current, a time when you were really thirsty but had nothing to drink, learning that someone had drowned?

Water is life giving and death dealing. Without water we cannot live, but water can also bring danger and death. We use water in Baptism because Baptism is also about life and death—death to sin that separates us from God and the birth of a new life in the Holy Spirit. Consider these words from the Letter to the Romans that are proclaimed at the Easter Vigil:

> Do you not know that all of us who have been baptized into Christ Jesus were baptized into his death? Therefore we have been buried with him by baptism into death, so that, just as Christ was raised from the dead by the glory of the Father, so we too might walk in newness of life. . . .
>
> So you also must consider yourselves dead to sin and alive to God in Christ Jesus. (Romans 6:3–4,11)

Living for God

The time of preparation for Confirmation is also a time for remembering your own Baptism and thinking about its meaning for your life now and in the future. If your Baptism took place when you were too young to remember it, ask your parents, godparents, or other family members to share stories about it.

Bible bytes

Jesus [said], "Very truly, I tell you, no one can enter the kingdom of God without being born of water and Spirit. What is born of the flesh is flesh, and what is born of the Spirit is spirit. Do not be astonished that I said to you, 'You must be born from above.' The wind blows where it chooses, and you hear the sound of it, but you do not know where it comes from or where it goes. So it is with everyone who is born of the Spirit."

—John 3:5–8

As a deer longs for flowing streams,
    so my soul longs for you, O God.
My soul thirsts for God,
    for the living God.

—Psalm 42:1–2

The Baptisms of most Catholics your age involved the following actions. First, your parents presented you for Baptism by announcing your name and stating that they were seeking Baptism for you. Then the celebrant asked your parents to accept responsibility for bringing you up to keep God's commandments by loving God and neighbor. After your godparents agreed to help your parents, the celebrant traced the sign of the cross on your forehead and invited your parents and godparents to do the same. This was a sign of their willingness to nurture your faith life and a sign of your new identity as a Christian. Your parents and godparents also expressed willingness to nurture your life of faith by renewing the vows of their own Baptism. They rejected Satan and professed faith in Jesus Christ.

At the heart of the sacrament of Baptism is the water bath. The name of the sacrament comes from the Greek *baptizein*, which means "to plunge" or "to immerse." The celebrant immersed you in blessed water or poured the water over your head three times while saying these words from the rite of Baptism, "[Name], I baptize you in the name of the Father, and of the Son, and of the Holy Spirit." Through Baptism you were freed from sin and incorporated into the Church. You were given a new life in the Holy Spirit.

After the water bath, several additional ritual actions took place, which help to explain what had happened. You were anointed with sacred chrism, signifying that you were given the gift of the Holy Spirit. You were dressed in white, signifying that you had risen with Christ and become a new creation. A candle was lit for you from the Easter candle, signifying that you had been enlightened by Christ. Your light was entrusted to your parents and godparents, who assumed responsibility for keeping the flame of faith burning in your heart.

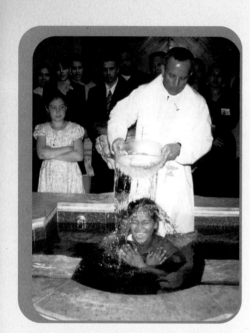

The LORD is my shepherd, I shall not want.
. . . .
he leads me beside still waters;
  he restores my soul.

—Psalm 23:1–3

Baptism: New Life in Christ

Catholic Connection Here are just a few of Baptism's major effects (with relevant paragraphs from the *Catechism* given in parentheses after each one):

> All sins are forgiven, original sin and all personal sins, as well as any punishment that might be attached to them. (Number 1263)

> We become adopted children of God, members of Christ's Body, and temples of the Holy Spirit. (Number 1265)

> We are incorporated into the Church. As Saint Paul put it, "For in the one Spirit we were all baptized into one body." (1 Corinthians 12:13; number 1267)

> We receive the power to live and act under the guidance of the Holy Spirit. (Number 1266)

> We are sealed with an indelible spiritual mark indicating that we belong to Christ. For this reason, a person celebrates Baptism only once. (Number 1272)

For all those reasons and more, Baptism is required for salvation "for those to whom the Gospel has been proclaimed and who have had the possibility of asking for this sacrament[13]" (number 1257).

Renewing the Promises of My Baptism

During your Confirmation you will be asked by the bishop to stand with your fellow candidates and renew the promises that were recited at your Baptism. We promise, in a sense, to "live into our Baptism." The baptismal promises, probably made on your behalf by your godparents and parents, are offered below in adapted form. The adaptation is made both to clarify the meaning of the vows and to preserve the special significance of the renewal of vows at your Confirmation.

Please respond as indicated while your leader guides the renewal of vows.

Leader: In anticipation of your Confirmation, please indicate your readiness to renew the vows made at your Baptism. Will you reject the power of evil and all its manifestations, both in your own life and in society?

Candidate's response: I will.

Leader: Will you affirm your belief in God the Father, the Creator and Lord of the universe, the Source of all that is?

Response: I will.

Leader: Will you once again profess your faith in Jesus Christ, God's only Son and our Lord, who was born of the Virgin Mary, who with the Father in the unity of the Holy Spirit, established the Reign of God, who died on the cross, and who was then raised to life and glorified by God the Father in heaven?

Response: I will.

Heart link

All-powerful God, Father of our Lord Jesus Christ, by water and the Holy Spirit you freed your sons and daughters from sin and gave them new life.

—From the rite of Confirmation

Bible byte "I am the bread of life. Whoever comes to me will never be hungry, and whoever believes in me will never be thirsty."

—John 6:35

Leader: Will you proclaim your belief in the Holy Spirit, one with the Father and the Son, Jesus Christ, in the Trinity, who came upon the Apostles at Pentecost and who on that day will shower God's graces on you in Confirmation?

Response: I will.

Leader: Will you proclaim your belief in the universal Church; the communion of believers, both living and dead; profess the forgiveness of God for all past offenses; and look with hope to that future day when you will be welcomed into resurrected life in heaven?

Response: I will.

Leader: This renewal of vows sums up the heart of our faith as Christians. We accept and celebrate that faith with believers throughout the world. We profess that faith with pride and with confidence in the One who revealed it to us, Jesus the Christ and our Lord.

Response: Amen.

CATHOLIC CONNECTION

The following prayer is taken from the Easter Vigil liturgy, when the baptismal water is blessed as a reminder of our own baptism:

Lord our God,

this night your people keep prayerful vigil.

Be with us as we recall the wonder of our creation

and the greater wonder of our redemption.

Bless this water: it makes the seed to grow,

it refreshes us and makes us clean.

You have made of it a servant of your loving kindness:

through water you set your people free,

and quenched their thirst in the desert.

With water the prophets announced a new covenant

that you would make with man.

By water, made holy by Christ in the Jordan,

You made our sinful nature new

in the bath that gives rebirth.

Let this water remind us of our baptism.

—*Sacramentary,* page 203

Your Baptism

Imagine your Baptism. Though you may have been too young at the time to remember it, try to create a picture in your mind. How old were you? Where was the Baptism celebrated? Who was with you? What happened during the celebration? How do you think your family felt about your Baptism? What kinds of hopes and prayers did they have for you?

Now spend a few minutes thinking about all the time that has passed since your Baptism and consider this question: What difference has being baptized made in your life? Jot down your reflections.

The Eucharist: Nourished Through the Holy Spirit

Bible byte "Abide in me as I abide in you. . . . I am the vine, you are the branches. Those who abide in me and I in them bear much fruit, because apart from me you can do nothing. . . . As the Father has loved me, so I have loved you; abide in my love."

—John 15:4–9

Catechism quote What material food produces in our bodily life, Holy Communion wonderfully achieves in our spiritual life.

—*Catechism,* no. 1392

While celebrating the Jewish feast of Passover with his disciples, Jesus "took a loaf of bread, and when he had given thanks, he broke it and gave it to them, saying, 'This is my body, which is given for you. Do this in remembrance of me.' And he did the same with the cup after supper, saying, 'This cup that is poured out for you is the new covenant in my blood'" (Luke 22:19–20).

When we celebrate the sacrament of the Eucharist, we do so "in remembrance of" Jesus and in thanksgiving (*eucharist* means "thanksgiving") for all he has done for us, but our celebration is much more than remembering past events. In the Eucharist Jesus's saving actions—his life, death, and Resurrection—are made present through the power of the Holy Spirit. The Eucharist makes Jesus's sacrifice on the cross present and unites us to it. Our celebrations of the Eucharist bring Jesus's death and Resurrection right into our midst and enable us to live out this mystery—called the Paschal mystery—in our own lives.

In the Eucharist simple gifts of bread and wine are consecrated. This conversion of the bread and wine into the body and blood of Jesus Christ is called transubstantiation. The bread and wine are transformed by God into nourishment for our spirit, transformed into Jesus Christ himself—into his body and blood, which God gives back to us to be shared as food and drink for the journey of life. Not only are the gifts of bread and wine changed in the Eucharist; everyone who participates is changed as well.

Parts of the Mass

Catholic Connection The Mass consists of four movements:

> **The Introductory Rites.** We gather together in community and prepare to celebrate the Eucharist. The introductory rites are all those that precede the liturgy of the word, including the entrance procession, the greeting, the opening prayer, a rite of penitence or a sprinkling rite, the Kyrie, the Gloria, and an opening prayer. Their purpose is to help us recognize Christ's presence and to prepare us to listen attentively to the readings and to fully participate in the Eucharist.

> **The Liturgy of the Word.** During the main part of the liturgy of the word, we hear the word of God proclaimed through Scripture readings and the responsorial psalm. After the proclamation of the Gospel, the presider gives a homily that explains the readings and urges us strongly to accept them as the word of God. The liturgy of the word concludes with the profession of faith (the creed) and the prayers of intercession.

> **The Liturgy of the Eucharist.** The preparation of the gifts of bread and wine marks the beginning of the liturgy of the Eucharist. The presider then leads us in the Eucharistic prayer, a prayer of thanksgiving and consecration that is the high point of the entire Mass. Then everyone participates in the Communion rite, which includes the Lord's Prayer, the sign of peace, the breaking of the bread, and the sharing of Communion.

> **The Dismissal Rite.** The presider blesses us and sends us forth to love and serve the Lord and one another. In other words, we are sent out to be the Body of Christ in the world and to live the meaning of what we have celebrated together.

Among the four parts of the Mass, the liturgy of the word and the liturgy of the Eucharist are the central ones. Together they form a single act of worship. The disciples' encounter with the risen Jesus on the road to Emmaus follows the same movement. While walking, Jesus explained the meaning of the Scriptures to them. Then, at table, "he took bread, blessed and broke it, and gave it to them" (Luke 24:30).

Spiritual Food and Drink

When we are hungry and thirsty, we yearn for food and drink to satisfy our most basic needs. Sometimes we speak of being hungry or thirsty in a figurative way, when we yearn for things such as God or justice or love. When we gather for the Eucharist, we hunger and thirst for a relationship with God and with one another. Communion with the Body and Blood of Christ strengthens the bond of charity with Christ.

Perhaps you wonder why we use bread and wine? The simple answer is, we use them because Jesus did at the Last Supper, and Jesus used them because the Jewish people did during meals, including Passover. Let's briefly explore the role of this food and drink in ancient Palestine.

 For I received from the Lord what I also handed on to you, that the Lord Jesus on the night when he was betrayed took a loaf of bread, and when he had given thanks, he broke it and said, "This is my body that is for you. Do this in remembrance of me." In the same way he took the cup also, after supper, saying, "This cup is the new covenant in my blood. Do this, as often as you drink it, in remembrance of me." For as often as you eat this bread and drink the cup, you proclaim the Lord's death until he comes.

—1 Corinthians 11:23–26

 Christ is always present in His Church, especially in her liturgical celebrations. He is present in the Sacrifice of the Mass not only in the person of His minister . . . but especially under the eucharistic species. . . . He is present in His word since it is He Himself who speaks when the holy scriptures are read in the Church. He is present, lastly, when the Church prays and sings, for He promised: "Where two or three are gathered together in my name, there am I in the midst of them" (Matthew 18:20).

—*Sacrosanctum Concilium*, no. 7

109

If we live by the Spirit, let us also be guided by the Spirit.

—Galatians 5:25

In Mediterranean culture during Jesus's earthly ministry, bread and wine were staples—the most basic food and drink used to satisfy physical hunger and thirst. Today we can draw on our own experience to understand that bread is a basic food eaten to satisfy hunger. Wine is a different story, of course, because we don't commonly drink it to satisfy thirst. In ancient Palestine, wine was the most plentiful drink, and it was readily available throughout the year. One reason for this was that the soil was very good for cultivating grapes. Another reason was the lack of availability of other drinks. Water was scarce in ancient Palestine, and milk, which turned sour without refrigeration, was most useful in solid form as cheese, yogurt, or curds.

Bread and wine are both gifts from God and products of human action. They are made from grain and grapes that come from the earth. Through human effort, including the crushing of the grain and the grapes, they become bread and wine. During Mass, at the beginning of the liturgy of the Eucharist, the community presents gifts of bread and wine. They are, as we pray, the fruit of the earth and the vine and the work of human hands. The bread and wine are gifts from God and symbols of ourselves and our cooperation with God's creation.

During the Eucharistic prayer, the priest prays over the bread and wine. On behalf of everyone gathered, the presider asks the Father to send the Holy Spirit upon the bread and wine and upon us so that we may be one body united through the Spirit. The bread that is broken and the wine that is poured out become the Body and Blood of Jesus Christ. When we receive Communion, we eat and drink more than ordinary bread and wine, which satisfies physical hunger and thirst. We also eat and drink that which satisfies our deepest spiritual hunger and thirst—the body and blood of Christ. Our communion with the Father and with one another nourishes us spiritually and strengthens us to go forth and make the love of God known in the world.

Sunday Eucharist is an obligatory holy day. The Sunday liturgy is sacramental, "God the Father is blessed and adored as the source of all the blessings of creation and salvation," the Holy Spirit prepares those assembled to encounter Christ, and through the gift of communion we are given the grace to bear fruit in the Church and the world (*Catechism*, numbers 1110–1112).

The Eucharist

Perhaps you feel bored at Mass sometimes and feel that your spiritual hunger and thirst is not satisfied. Perhaps you feel like you are simply part of an audience watching other people do things. Those are not reasons to stay home. Instead, this presents you with a challenge. You may need to spend some time preparing for Mass to help you pay closer attention to what is happening during it. Try reading the Scriptures a few days before Mass and thinking about what they mean to you. Or practice praying before Mass to quiet your thoughts and open yourself to the Holy Spirit. You may find that a little preparation helps you to more fully enter into the meaning of the words and actions of the Eucharist so that you might, with the grace of the Holy Spirit, live more fully the way of life modeled by Jesus.

Jesus's challenge to "do this in memory of me" is nothing less than the challenge of putting your whole self into the celebration of the Eucharist and the Christian life. Jesus's promise is that the Holy Spirit will fill your whole being and satisfy your hunger and thirst.

Hungry and thirsty for God

Think for a moment about all that you hunger and thirst for in your life. Jot some notes in the space below. Review the list and identify the items on your list that are spiritual needs. Reflect on how your spiritual hunger and thirst can be satisfied through the Eucharist.

Confirmation:
Sealed with the Holy Spirit

When you are confirmed the bishop will anoint you by tracing the sign of the cross on your forehead with holy chrism. He will say your name and the words "Be sealed with the gift of the Holy Spirit." This anointing is a sign of a spiritual anointing. Through this sacrament you receive a priceless gift, a special outpouring of the Holy Spirit, who gives you special strength to live as a Christian and to be a witness of Christ through your words and your actions.

To be "sealed" signifies that you have received a permanent, spiritual imprint indicating that you belong completely to Jesus Christ through the Holy Spirit.

The holy chrism used in Confirmation is olive oil mixed with balsam, which perfumes the oil and signifies joy. The oil extracted from the fruit of the olive tree is rich in symbolism because of its many uses across thousands of years of history. Some of the uses are to cleanse the body, to limber the body in preparation for athletic events, as a fuel for lamps, to soothe wounds and bruises, as a cosmetic to make a person shine with radiance, and as a basic part of the diet. The Book of Sirach, written early in the second century BC, includes oil in a list of life's necessities: "water and fire and iron and salt and wheat flour and milk and honey, the blood of the grape and oil and cloth-ing" (Sirach 39:26). In the Old Testament, olive oil is a sign of God's abun-dant love.

The ritual use of oil to anoint people or things for religious purposes dates back to ancient times. Priests and kings, for example, were anointed as they assumed their positions, as a sign that God was with them. The meaning of the anointing in the sacrament of Confirmation today is rooted in this histo-ry; however, it specifically signifies our bond with Christ and the Church and the gift of a special strength that makes us better able to assume the respon-sibilities of the Christian life. Through the grace of Baptism and Confirmation, we share in Christ's priesthood: ever more united with him in holiness to live out our Christian vocation in our personal, family, social, and ecclesial lives.

Confirmation increases and deepens the grace we received at Baptism. Through Confirmation we are strengthened by the Holy Spirit to better live out our Christian vocation. Our unity with Christ becomes firmer and our

Bible byte I remind you to rekindle the gift of God that is within you through the laying on of my hands; for God did not give us a spir-it of cowardice, but rather a spirit of power and of love and of self-discipline.

—2 Timothy 1:6–7

connection with the Church grows stronger. Everyone is encouraged to celebrate Confirmation because the special outpouring of the Holy Spirit completes our Baptism. Without Confirmation and the Eucharist, a baptized person's Christian initiation remains incomplete. Our celebration of Confirmation during the Eucharist emphasizes the unity of the sacraments of initiation.

Gifts of the Holy Spirit

Before you are anointed, the bishop will say a special prayer for you and the others being confirmed. He and all the priests who are present lay hands on you by extending their hands over the whole group while the bishop says these words:

Bible byte [John the Baptist] proclaimed, "The one who is more powerful than I is coming after me; I am not worthy to stoop down and untie the thong of his sandals. I have baptized you with water; but he will baptize you with the Holy Spirit."

—Mark 1:7–8

Heart link Beware of supposing that this ointment is mere ointment. Just as after the invocation of the Holy Spirit, the Eucharistic bread is no longer ordinary bread, but the Body of Christ, so this holy oil, in conjunction with the invocation, is no longer simple or common oil, but becomes the gracious gift of Christ and the Holy Spirit.

—Saint Cyril of Jerusalem

All-powerful God, Father of our Lord Jesus Christ,

by water and the Holy Spirit

you freed your sons and daughters from sin

and gave them new life.

Send your Holy Spirit upon them

to be their Helper and Guide.

Give them the spirit of wisdom and understanding,

the spirit of right judgment and courage,

the spirit of knowledge and reverence.

Fill them with the spirit of wonder and awe in

your presence.

We ask this through Christ our Lord.

Amen.

—From the rite of Confirmation

The bishop and priests use the gesture of laying on hands because it represents the gesture used in the Scriptures to invoke, or call, the Holy Spirit. After Pentecost the Apostles gave the gift of the Holy Spirit to others through this gesture. The words of the prayer ask the Father to send the Spirit and to shower gifts on everyone being confirmed.

The Church has traditionally spoken of the seven gifts of the Holy Spirit: wisdom, understanding, right judgment, courage, knowledge, reverence, and wonder and awe.

> **Wisdom.** Through wisdom, the wonders of nature, every event in history, and all the ups and downs of our life take on deeper meaning and purpose. The wise person sees where the Holy Spirit is at work and is able to share that insight with others. Wisdom is the fullest expression of the gifts of knowledge and understanding.

> **Understanding.** The gift of understanding is the ability to comprehend how a person must live his or her life as a follower of Jesus. Through the gift of understanding, Christians realize that the Gospel tells them not just who Jesus is; it also tells them who we are. The gift of understanding is closely related to the gifts of knowledge and wisdom.

> **Right judgment.** The gift of right judgment is the ability to know the difference between right and wrong and then to choose what is good. It helps us to act on and live out what Jesus has taught. In the exercise of right judgment, many of the other gifts—especially understanding, wisdom, and often courage—come into play in the Christian's daily life.

> **Courage.** The gift of courage enables us to take risks and to overcome fear as we try to live out the Gospel of Jesus. Followers of Jesus confront many challenges and even danger—the risk of being laughed at, the fear of rejection, and, for some believers, the fear of physical harm and even death. The Holy Spirit gives Christians the strength to confront and ultimately overcome such challenges.

> **Knowledge.** The gift of knowledge is the ability to comprehend the basic meaning and message of Jesus Christ. Jesus revealed the will of his Father, and taught people what they need to know to achieve fullness of life and ultimately salvation. The gift of knowledge is closely related to the gifts of understanding and wisdom.

> **Reverence.** Sometimes called piety, the gift of reverence gives the Christian a deep sense of respect for God. Jesus spoke of his Father as "Abba," an intimate name similar to "Daddy" or "Papa." Through the gift of reverence, we can come before the Father with the openness and trust of small children, totally dependent on the One who created us.

> **Wonder and awe.** The gift of wonder and awe in the presence of God is sometimes translated as "the fear of the Lord." Though we can approach God with the trust of little children, we are also often aware of God's total majesty, unlimited power, and desire for justice. A child may want to sit on the lap of his loving Father, but sometimes the believer will fall on her or his knees in the presence of the Creator of the universe.

These gifts are rooted in a prophecy in Isaiah about the coming Messiah: "The spirit of the LORD shall rest on him, the spirit of wisdom and understanding, the spirit of counsel and might, the spirit of knowledge and the fear of the LORD" (11:2–3). Over time the Church started to use these named gifts as symbolic or representative of the totality of gifts (in the Bible, the number seven represents fullness or completion) that the Holy Spirit constantly showers on all people of faith.

The gifts of the Holy Spirit are activated, at least in potential, in the life of each Christian at his or her Baptism. In and through Confirmation, the full power of those gifts is unleashed. The individual accepting Confirmation, with the support of the community of faith, experiences an increased ability to walk in the way of Jesus.

The gifts of the Holy Spirit are not magic. You will not "get more God" through the sacraments. God will not love you more the day after Confirmation, for example, than the day before. Nevertheless, any time we open ourselves to the work of God's grace, particularly within the context of the Church's sacramental celebrations, the grace of God becomes more active, evident, and effective in our life.

The Church also speaks of the fruits of the Holy Spirit, the good things that result when we allow ourselves to be guided by the Spirit. The fruits of the Holy Spirit are "charity, joy, peace, patience, kindness, goodness, generosity, gentleness, faithfulness, modesty, self-control, chastity" (*Catechism*, number 1832). When you live by the Spirit, do you notice those things becoming more present in your life?

Consecration of the Chrism

The bishop consecrates the chrism for his whole diocese at a special Mass, called the Chrism Mass, celebrated on Holy Thursday. The bishop introduces the prayer of consecration by inviting everyone gathered to pray that God will bless the oil and that all who are anointed with it will be transformed and will share in eternal life. Here is an excerpt from one of the prayers used to consecrate chrism:

And so, Father, we ask you to bless this oil you have created. Fill it with the power of your Holy Spirit through Christ your Son. It is from him that chrism takes its name and with chrism you have anointed for yourself priests and kings, prophets and martyrs.

Make this chrism a sign of life and salvation for those who are to be born again in the waters of baptism. Wash away the evil they have inherited from sinful Adam, and when they are anointed with this holy oil, make them temples of your glory, radiant with the goodness of life that has its source in you.

Through this sign of chrism grant them royal, priestly, prophetic honor, and clothe them with incorruption. Let this be indeed the chrism of salvation for those who will be born again of water and the Holy Spirit. May they come to share eternal life in the glory of your kingdom. We ask this through Christ our Lord. Amen.

—From the rite of consecrating the chrism, number 25

The consecration of the chrism is an important action that is, in a sense, considered part of the celebration of Confirmation.

What Confirmation means to me

In this session you have been introduced to key elements of the rite of Confirmation. Based on what you have learned, and given your past and present relationship with the Church, jot down here your current hopes and wishes for your relationship with the Church as a confirmed member.

Confirmation: Celebrating the Rite

Confirmation is almost here . . . finally! The journey of preparation has been a demanding one. You may be able to identify with some of the feelings expressed in Paul's letter to the Philippians:

> Not that I have already obtained . . . the goal; but I press on to make it my own, because Christ Jesus has made me his own. Beloved, I do not consider that I have made it my own; but this one thing I do: forgetting what lies behind and straining forward to what lies ahead, I press on toward the goal.
>
> —Philippians 3:12–14

It's now time to prepare for the final step of the journey, to "press on toward the goal"—the rite of Confirmation—and a life of full participation in the Church's mission. This session is designed to help you fully understand, participate in, and enjoy the celebration of the sacrament.

Summing Up

Your journey of preparation for Confirmation has covered a lot of ground. The *Catechism* offers a list of the effects of Confirmation that summarizes well what you and your fellow candidates have studied, discussed, and prayed over during the process of preparation (see numbers 1303–1304):

> ❯ We have stressed the close link between Confirmation and Baptism. In Confirmation we affirm and deepen our Baptism and strengthen the relationship to the Triune God that our Baptism initiated and celebrated.

> ❯ Confirmation increases and deepens baptismal grace. In fact, "Confirmation is necessary for the completion of baptismal grace[14]" (*Catechism*, number 1285).

> ❯ Confirmation identifies us more deeply as children of God who with faith and joy can dare to call God our Father, "Abba."

> ❯ It unites us more firmly to Jesus Christ, whose message and mission we now embrace with freedom and fuller awareness.

> ❯ Confirmation ignites within us the gifts of the Holy Spirit that were showered on us at Baptism.

> ❯ It more deeply bonds us to the Church, the Body of Christ.

Heart link All-powerful God

. . . .

Fill them with the spirit of wonder and awe in your presence.

—From the rite of Confirmation

Bible byte "If you love me, you will keep my commandments. And I will ask the Father, and he will give you another Advocate, to be with you forever. This is the Spirit of truth, whom the world cannot receive, because it neither sees him nor knows him. You know him, because he abides with you, and he will be in you.

—John 14:15–17

> It awakens in our heart a passion to proclaim the Gospel by word and deed as disciples and witnesses of Jesus Christ.

> Confirmation, like Baptism, imprints an indelible spiritual mark on the soul, signifying that Jesus Christ has marked the confirmed person with the seal of his Spirit. For that reason Confirmation, like Baptism, is given only once.

As a candidate for Confirmation you now must "profess the faith, be in a state of grace, have the intention of receiving the sacrament, and be prepared to assume the role of disciple and witness to Christ," both within the community of faith and in society (*Catechism,* number 1319).

The *Catechism* quotes Saint Ambrose, whose words over sixteen hundred years ago serve as a fitting conclusion for the process of preparation:

Recall then that you have received the spiritual zeal, the spirit of wisdom and understanding, the spirit of right judgment and courage, the spirit of knowledge and reverence, the spirit of holy fear in God's presence. Guard what you have received. God the Father has marked you with his sign; Christ the Lord has confirmed you and has placed his pledge, the Spirit, in your hearts.[15] (Number 1303)

Amen!

Celebrating the Rite of Confirmation

Below is a description of the rite of Confirmation when it is celebrated within a Mass. Your leader will provide more specific details about your upcoming celebration of Confirmation. Also, you will likely walk through a practice session in preparation for the celebration of the rite.

> **Introductory rites.** Everyone gathers for the celebration. You and the other candidates and your sponsors may be invited to participate in the opening procession. If not, you and your sponsor will be seated prior to the procession in a specially designated area or with your family.

> **Liturgy of the word.** All will hear the word of God proclaimed. The readings will be those designated for the day on which Confirmation is celebrated or they will be specially selected from a list of readings suggested in the lectionary. "It is from the hearing of the word of God that the many-sided work of the Holy Spirit flows out upon the Church and upon each one of the baptized and confirmed" (*Rite of Confirmation,* number 13).

> **Presentation of the candidates.** A leader from your parish will present you and the other candidates to the bishop. Unless the size of the group prevents it, the person making the presentation will call your name.

> **Homily.** The liturgy of the word continues with the homily. The bishop will explain the readings and help the community come to a deeper understanding of the sacrament of Confirmation. At the end of the homily, he will ask you, along with all the other candidates, to profess your faith by renewing your baptismal promises.

> **Renewal of baptismal vows.** The renewal of these vows helps to express the close connection between Baptism and Confirmation. Your response, a series of "I do's," may appear simple, but the meaning is all-important. You denounce Satan and profess your belief in the Trinity—Father, Son, and Holy Spirit. After your profession, the bishop says: "This is our faith. This is the faith of the Church. We are proud to profess it in Christ Jesus our Lord." All the people gathered respond, "Amen."

> **Laying on of hands.** The bishop and the priests extend their hands over the whole group of candidates, a gesture that signifies the gift of the Holy Spirit. The bishop invokes the Holy Spirit using the prayer discussed during the last session. He prays to the Father, asking him to send his Holy Spirit upon you and the other candidates.

> **Anointing with chrism.** This is the heart of the sacrament of Confirmation. Your sponsor presents you to the bishop and places her or his right hand on your shoulder as a sign of support and commitment to helping you live faithfully. Then the bishop dips his right thumb in the chrism and traces the sign of the cross on your forehead, saying your name and the words, "Be sealed with the gift of the Holy Spirit." Your response is "Amen." After the anointing, you and the bishop will exchange a sign of peace. He will say to you, "Peace be with you." Your response is "And also with you." This gesture of peace is a sign of the bond or communion shared by all the faithful with one another and with the bishop.

> **General intercessions.** All join together in prayer. The community responds with "Lord, hear our prayer" or something similar.

> **Liturgy of the Eucharist.** The celebration of Confirmation is normally celebrated within a Mass. This helps to highlight the unity of the three sacraments of initiation and the communion shared among all the faithful with God.

The fruit of the Spirit is love, joy, peace, patience, kindness, generosity, faithfulness, gentleness, and self-control. . . . If we live by the Spirit, let us also be guided by the Spirit.

—Galatians 5:22–25

Life is a pilgrimage of discovery

For it is true to say that life is a pilgrimage of discovery: the discovery of who you are, the discovery of the values that shape your lives, the discovery of the peoples and nations to which all are bound in solidarity. While this voyage of discovery is most evident in the time of youth, it is a voyage that never ends. . . .

. . . The world needs young people who have drunk deeply of the sources of truth. . . . You must form in yourselves a deep sense of responsibility. . . .

. . . So do not be afraid to commit your lives to peace and justice, for you know that the Lord is with you in all ways.

—Pope John Paul II

Personal thoughts as Confirmation nears

In just a short time, you will be celebrating your Confirmation. As a sacrament, Confirmation was instituted by Christ. The visible rite of Confirmation that you will experience is a celebration that signifies and makes present the grace of divine life and will bear fruit in your life if your heart is properly disposed. This can and should be a prayerful time, an opportunity to gather your thoughts and feelings as you open your heart to the gifts of the Holy Spirit and deepen your relationship with the community of faith that welcomes you. Jot down here your reflections and hopes, perhaps in the form of a prayer to the Holy Spirit, as your Confirmation approaches.

e Universal Prayer

d, I believe you: increase my faith.
st in you: strengthen my trust.
e you: let me love you more
    and more.
n sorry for my sins: deepen
    my sorrow.

rship you as my first beginning,
ng for you as my last end,
aise you as my constant helper
d call on you as my loving protector.

de me by your wisdom,
rect me with your justice,
nfort me with your mercy,
tect me with your power.

fer you, Lord, my thoughts: to be
    fixed on you;
words: to have you for
    their theme;
actions to reflect my love for you;
sufferings: to be endured for your
    greater glory.

ant to do what you ask of me:
he way you ask,
as long as you ask
ause you ask it.

d, enlighten my understanding,
ength my will,
ify my heart,
d make me holy.

p me to repent of my past sins
d to resist temptation in the future.
p me to rise above my human
    weaknesses
d to grow stronger as a Christian.

me love you, my Lord and my God
d see myself as I really am:
ilgrim in this world,
Christian called to respect and love
whose lives I touch,
se in authority over me
those under my authority,
friends and my enemies.

Help me to conquer anger with
    gentleness,
Greed by generosity,
Apathy by fervor.
Help me to forget myself
And reach out toward others.

Make me prudent in planning,
Courageous in taking risks.
Make me patient in suffering,
    unassuming in prosperity

Keep me, Lord, attentive at prayer
Temperate in food and drink,
Diligent in my work,
Firm in my good intentions.

Let my conscience be clear,
My conduct without fault,
My speech blameless,
My life well-ordered.

Put me on guard against my human
    weaknesses.
Let me cherish your love for me,
Keep your law,
And come at last to your salvation.

Teach me to realize that this world
    is passing,
That my true future is the happiness
    of heaven,
That life on earth is short,
And life to come eternal.
Help me to prepare for death
With a proper fear of judgment,
But a greater trust in your goodness.
Lead me safely through death
To the endless joy of heaven.
Grant this through Christ our Lord.

Amen.

(This prayer, an adaptation of the original "The Universal Prayer" written by Pope Clement XI, is at "Prayers for All Christians," *www.rc.net/wcc/ univpray.htm*, accessed September 22, 2005.)

Heart link Do not be afraid of the risks! God's strength is always far more powerful than your difficulties! . . . Much more influential than the corruption present in the world is the divine power of the Sacrament of Confirmation, which brings Baptism to its maturity. And incomparably greater than all is the power of the Eucharist.

—Pope John Paul II

Catholic Quick Facts

Catholic Quick Facts is a mini-encyclopedia of basic information on Catholicism.
In these pages you will find the following sections:

Catholic Beliefs and Practices

In using this collection of major Catholic beliefs and practices, be aware of two things:

- Many of the items that are only listed here are more fully defined in the glossary of Catholic terms and definitions. For example, here we list the seven Catholic sacraments; in the glossary of terms, we define each one.

- Behind many of these items, you will see a number in parentheses. That number refers to a paragraph in the *Catechism of the Catholic Church*. The referenced paragraph is often just the beginning of a complete discussion of the item that we can only briefly name here. If you would like more information on any of these beliefs and practices, look to the *Catechism* as a primary reference.

Two Great Commandments

- You shall love the Lord your God with all your heart, with all your soul, and all your mind, and with all your strength.

- You shall love your neighbor as yourself.

(Matthew 22:37–40, Mark 12:29–31, Luke 10:27)

Ten Commandments
(see *Catechism*, number 2084 and following)

1. I am the Lord your God: you shall not have strange gods before me.
2. You shall not take the name of the Lord, your God, in vain.
3. Remember to keep holy the Lord's Day.
4. Honor your father and mother.
5. You shall not kill.
6. You shall not commit adultery.
7. You shall not steal.
8. You shall not bear false witness against your neighbor.

9. You shall not covet your neighbor's wife.
10. You shall not covet your neighbor's goods.

Beatitudes
(see *Catechism*, number 1716)

- Blessed are the poor in spirit, the kingdom of heaven is theirs.
- Blessed are they who mourn, they will be comforted.
- Blessed are the meek, they will inherit the earth.
- Blessed are they who hunger and thirst for righteousness, they will be satisfied.
- Blessed are the merciful, they will be shown mercy.
- Blessed are the clean of heart, they will see God.
- Blessed are the peacemakers, they will be called children of God.
- Blessed are they who are persecuted for the sake of righteousness, the kingdom of heaven is theirs.

Corporal Works of Mercy
(see *Catechism*, number 2447)

- Feed the hungry.
- Give drink to the thirsty.
- Shelter the homeless.
- Clothe the naked.
- Care for the sick.
- Help the imprisoned.
- Bury the dead.

Spiritual Works of Mercy
(see *Catechism*, number 2447)

- Share knowledge.
- Give advice to those who need it.
- Comfort those who suffer.
- Be patient with others.
- Forgive those who hurt you.
- Give correction to those who need it.
- Pray for the living and the dead.

Theological Virtues
(see *Catechism*, number 1813)

- Faith
- Hope
- Love

Cardinal Virtues
(see *Catechism*, number 1805)

- Prudence
- Justice
- Fortitude
- Temperance

Seven Gifts of the Holy Spirit
(see *Catechism*, number 1831)

- *Wisdom.* Through wisdom, the wonders of nature, every event in history, and all the ups and downs of our life take on deeper meaning and purpose. The wise person sees where the Spirit of God is at work and is able to share that insight with others. Wisdom is the fullest expression of the gifts of knowledge and understanding.

- *Understanding.* The gift of understanding is the ability to comprehend how a person must live her or his life as a follower of Jesus. Through the gift of understanding, Christians realize that the Gospel tells them not just who Jesus is; it also tells them who we are. The gift of understanding is closely related to the gifts of knowledge and wisdom.

- *Right judgment.* The gift of right judgment is the ability to know the difference between right and wrong and then to choose what is good. It helps us to act on and live out what Jesus has taught. In the exercise of right judgment, many of the other gifts—especially understanding, wisdom, and often courage—come into play in the Christian's daily life.

- *Courage.* The gift of courage enables us to take risks and to overcome fear as we try to live out the Gospel of Jesus. Followers of Jesus confront many challenges and even danger—the risk of being laughed at, the fear of rejection, and, for some believers, the fear of physical harm and even death. The Spirit gives Christians the strength to confront and ultimately overcome such challenges.

- *Knowledge.* The gift of knowledge is the ability to comprehend the basic meaning and message of Jesus. Jesus revealed the will of God, his Father, and taught people what they need to know to achieve fullness of life and, ultimately, salvation. The gift of knowledge is closely related to the gifts of understanding and wisdom.

- *Reverence.* Sometimes called piety, the gift of reverence gives the Christian a deep sense of respect for God. Jesus spoke of his Father, God, as "Abba," a very intimate name similar to "daddy" or "papa." Through the gift of reverence, we can come before God with the openness and trust of small children, totally dependent on the One who created us.

- *Wonder and awe.* The gift of wonder and awe in the presence of God is sometimes translated as "the fear of the Lord." Though we can approach God with the trust of little children, we are also often aware of God's total majesty, unlimited power, and desire for justice. A child may want to sit on the lap of his loving Father, but sometimes the believer will fall on her knees in the presence of the Creator of the universe.

Fruits of the Holy Spirit
(see *Catechism*, number 1832)

- Charity
- Joy
- Peace
- Patience
- Goodness
- Kindness
- Long suffering
- Humility

- Faithfulness
- Modesty
- Continence
- Chastity

Four Marks of the Catholic Church
(see *Catechism*, number 750)

- One
- Holy
- Catholic
- Apostolic

Liturgical Year

- Advent
- Christmas
- Ordinary Time
- Lent
- Easter Triduum
- Easter
- Pentecost
- Ordinary Time

Seven Sacraments
(see *Catechism*, number 1210)

- Baptism
- Confirmation
- the Eucharist
- Penance and Reconciliation
- Anointing of the Sick
- Matrimony
- Holy Orders

Precepts of the Church
(see *Catechism*, numbers 2042–2043)

1. To keep holy the day of the Lord's Resurrection; to worship God by participating in Mass every Sunday and on the holy days of obligation; to avoid those activities that would hinder renewal of the soul and body on the Sabbath (for example, needless work or unnecessary shopping).

2. To lead a sacramental life; to receive Holy Communion frequently and the sacrament of Reconciliation regularly—minimally, to receive the sacrament of Reconciliation at least once a year (annual confession is obligatory only if serious sin is involved); minimally also, to receive Holy Communion at least once a year between the first Sunday of Lent and Trinity Sunday.

3. To study Catholic teaching in preparation for the sacrament of Confirmation, to be confirmed, and then to continue to study and advance the cause of Christ.

4. To observe the marriage laws of the Church; to give religious training, by example and word, to one's children; to use parish schools and catechetical programs.

5. To strengthen and support the Church—one's own parish community and parish priests, the worldwide Church, and the Pope.

6. To do penance, including abstaining from meat and fasting from food on the appointed days.

7. To join in the missionary spirit and apostolate (work) of the Church.

Holy Days of Obligation

- Christmas (December 25)
- Solemnity of the Blessed Virgin Mary, the Mother of God (January 1)
- Ascension of the Lord (the Sunday that follows forty days after Easter)
- Assumption of the Blessed Virgin Mary (August 15)
- All Saints (November 1)
- Immaculate Conception of the Blessed Virgin Mary (December 8)

Regulations on Fasting and Abstinence

The Catholic Church requires its members to observe certain dietary rules—fasting and abstinence—in order to recognize and mark the importance of particular days during its liturgical year, as well as to express penance for personal sin. The regulations apply as follows:

- Generally, the laws of fasting require that on the designated days the person eat just one full meal, two smaller meals, and avoid eating between meals. Abstinence laws require that the person avoid meat altogether.

- The regulations governing abstinence from meat apply to all Catholics age fourteen and older. Adults who have completed their eighteenth year until the beginning of their sixtieth year are bound by the regulations that govern fasting. Pregnant women and sick people are excused from the regulations.

- Ash Wednesday and Good Friday are days of both fasting and abstinence; all the other Fridays of Lent are days of abstinence only.

- In addition, the Church encourages its adult members to observe some form of penance, perhaps including some kind of fast and abstinence, on all Fridays throughout the year.

- The Church also calls for fasting prior to receiving Communion during the Mass. In this case, the fast helps us prepare our mind and heart for the great gift of the Eucharist by doing something physical to help focus our attention. Church law calls for us to avoid all food and drink, with the exception of water and medicine, for one hour before receiving Communion. Again, this regulation does not apply to sick people or others for whom such restrictions would jeopardize health.

Parts of the Mass
(see *Catechism*, number 1346)

Introductory Rites
- Entrance
- Act of Penitence
- Kyrie
- Gloria
- Collect (opening prayer)

Liturgy of the Word
- First Reading
- Responsorial Psalm
- Second Reading
- Gospel Acclamation
- Gospel Reading
- Homily
- Profession of Faith
- Prayers of the Faithful

Liturgy of the Eucharist
- Preparation of the Altar and the Gifts
- Prayers over the Gifts
- Eucharistic Prayer
- Communion Rite: Lord's Prayer
  Rite of Peace
  Breaking of the Bread
  Communion
  Silence/Song of Praise
- Prayer After Communion

Concluding Rites
- Greeting and Blessing
- Dismissal

Catholic Prayers and Devotions

As in the section on Catholic beliefs and practices, you will see a number in parentheses behind some of these prayers and devotions. That number refers you to a paragraph in the *Catechism of the Catholic Church* that may offer a more complete explanation of the prayer or devotion.

Act of Contrition
(see *Catechism,* number 1451)

My God, I am sorry for my sins
with all my heart, and I detest them.
In choosing to do wrong and failing to do good,
I have sinned against you,
whom I should love above all things.
I firmly intend, with your help,
to do penance, to sin no more,
and to avoid whatever leads me to sin.
Our savior Jesus Christ suffered and died for us.
In his name, my God, have mercy.

Act of Faith
My God, I firmly believe you are one God in
    three Divine Persons, Father, Son, and Holy
    Spirit.
I believe in Jesus Christ, your son, who became
    man and died for our sins, and who will
    come to judge the living and the dead.
I believe these and all the truths which theHoly
    Catholic Church teaches, because you have
    revealed them, who can neither deceive
    nor be deceived. Amen.

Act of Hope
O my God, trusting in your infinite goodness and promises, I hope to obtain pardon of my sins, the help of your grace, and life everlasting, through the merits of Jesus Christ, my Lord and redeemer. Amen.

Act of Love
My God, I love you above all things, with my whole heart and soul, because you are all-good and worthy of all my love. I love my neighbor as myself for love of you. I forgive all who have injured me, and I ask pardon of all whom I have injured. Amen.

Angelus
The angel of the Lord declared unto Mary,
And she conceived of the Holy Spirit.
    Hail Mary . . .
Behold the handmaid of the Lord,
Be it done unto me according to your word.
    Hail Mary . . .
And the Word was made flesh,
And dwelt among us.
    Hail Mary . . .
Pray for us, O Holy Mother of God, that we may be made worthy of the promises of Christ. Let us pray: Pour forth, we beseech you, O Lord, your grace into our hearts that we to whom the incarnation of Christ, your Son, was made known by the message of an angel may, by his passion and cross, be brought to the glory of his resurrection, through Christ our Lord.

Apostles' Creed
(see *Catechism,* numbers 194, 197, and following)
I believe in God, the Father Almighty, creator of heaven and earth. I believe in Jesus Christ, his only son, our Lord. He was conceived by the power of the Holy Spirit, and born of the Virgin Mary. He suffered under Pontius Pilate, was crucified, died, and was buried. He descended to the dead. On the third day he rose again. He ascended into heaven and is seated at the right hand of the Father. He will come again to judge the living and the dead.

I believe in the Holy Spirit, the holy catholic Church, the communion of saints, the forgiveness of sins, the resurrection of the body, and life everlasting. Amen.

Confiteor (I Confess)

I confess to almighty God, and to you, my brothers and sisters, that I have sinned through my own fault in my thoughts and in my words, in what I have done and what I have failed to do; and I ask blessed Mary, ever virgin, all the angels and saints, and you, my brothers and sisters, to pray for me to the Lord our God. May almighty God have mercy on us, forgive us our sins, and bring us to everlasting life.

Glory Be

Glory be to the Father, and to the Son, and to the Holy Spirit, as it was in the beginning, is now, and will be forever. Amen.

Grace Before Meals

Bless us, O Lord, and these your gifts,
which we are about to receive
from your bounty,
through Christ our Lord. Amen.

Grace After Meals

We give you thanks, almighty God,
for these and all your gifts
which we have received
through Christ our Lord. Amen.

Hail Mary

(see *Catechism*, numbers 2676–2677)

Hail Mary, full of grace,
the Lord is with you;
blessed are you among women,
and blessed is the fruit of your womb, Jesus.

Holy Mary, Mother of God,
pray for us sinners
now and at the hour of our death.
Amen.

The Lord's Prayer (also called the Our Father)

(see *Catechism*, number 2759)

Our Father who art in heaven,
hallowed be thy name.
Thy kingdom come.
Thy will be done on earth, as it is in heaven.
Give us this day our daily bread,
and forgive us our trespasses,
as we forgive those who trespass against us,
and lead us not into temptation,
but deliver us from evil. Amen.

Magnificat (Mary's Song)

(see Luke 1:46–55)

My being proclaims the greatness of the Lord,
my spirit finds joy in God my savior.
For he has looked upon his servant
in all her lowliness.
All ages to come shall call me blessed.
God who is mighty
has done great things for me, holy is his name;
his mercy is from age to age
on those who fear him.
He has shown might with his arm;
he has confused the proud
in their inmost thoughts.
He has deposed the mighty from their thrones
and raised the lowly to high places.

The hungry he has given every good thing
while the rich he has sent empty away.
He has upheld Israel his servant,
ever mindful of his mercy,
even as he promised our fathers,
promised Abraham and his descendants
forever.

Memorare

Remember, O most gracious Virgin Mary, that never was it known that anyone who fled to your protection, implored your help, or sought your intercession was left unaided. Inspired by this confidence, we fly unto you, O virgin of virgins, our mother. To you do we come, before you we stand, sinful and sorrowful. O mother of the Word Incarnate, despise not our petitions, but in your mercy, hear and answer us.

Morning Prayer

Almighty God, I thank you for your past blessings. Today I offer myself—whatever I do, say, or think—to your loving care. Continue to bless me, Lord. I make this morning offering in union with the divine intentions of Jesus Christ who offers himself daily in the holy sacrifice of the Mass, and in union with Mary, his Virgin Mother and our Mother, who was always the faithful handmaid of the Lord. Amen.

Prayer of Saint Francis

Lord, make me an instrument of your peace:
> where there is hatred, let me sow love;
> where there is injury, pardon;
> where there is doubt, faith;
> where there is despair, hope;
> where there is darkness, light;
> where there is sadness, joy.

Divine Master,
> grant that I may not so much seek
> to be consoled as to console,
> to be understood as to understand,
> to be loved as to love.

For it is in giving that we receive,
> it is in pardoning that we are pardoned,
> it is in dying that we are born to eternal life.

Prayer to the Holy Spirit
(see *Catechism*, number 2671)

Come, Holy Spirit, fill the hearts of your faithful. Enkindle in them the fire of your love. Send forth your Spirit, and they will be created. And you will renew the face of the earth.

Let us pray:

Lord, by the light of the Holy Spirit, you have taught the hearts of the faithful. In the same Spirit, help to us relish what is right and always rejoice in your consolation. We ask this through Christ our Lord. Amen.

The Rosary
(see *Catechism*, number 971)

The rosary is perhaps the most popular devotion to Mary, the Mother of God. The central part of the rosary consists of the recitation of five sets of ten Hail Marys (each set is called a decade). Each new decade begins by saying an Our Father, and each decade concludes with a Glory Be. The prayer keeps track of the prayers said by moving from one bead to the next in order.

The recitation of the rosary begins with a series of prayers, said in the following order while using as a guide a small chain of beads and a crucifix.

1. the sign of the cross
2. the Apostles' Creed
3. one Our Father
4. three Hail Marys
5. one Glory Be

After these introductory prayers, the recitation of the decades, as described above, begins.

The saying of a five-decade rosary is connected with meditation on what are called the mysteries of the life of Jesus. These mysteries too are collected into series of five—five joyful, five sorrowful, five glorious, and five luminous mysteries (recently added by Pope John Paul II). The mysteries of the rosary are listed below. The prayer devotes one recitation of the rosary to each set of mysteries. She or he chooses which set of mysteries to meditate on while saying the decades of Hail Marys. Therefore, the complete rosary consists of twenty decades.

With a little practice, the regular praying of the rosary can become a source of great inspiration and consolation for the Christian.

Joyful Mysteries
- The Annunciation
- The Visitation
- The Birth of Our Lord
- The Presentation of Jesus in the Temple
- The Finding of Jesus in the Temple

Sorrowful Mysteries
- The Agony of Jesus in the Garden
- The Scourging at the Pillar
- The Crowning of Thorns
- The Carrying of the Cross
- The Crucifixion

Glorious Mysteries
- The Resurrection of Jesus
- The Ascension of Jesus into Heaven
- The Descent of the Holy Spirit on the Apostles (Pentecost)
- The Assumption of Mary into Heaven
- The Crowning of Mary as Queen of Heaven

Luminous Mysteries
- The Baptism of Jesus
- Jesus Reveals Himself in the Miracle at Cana
- Jesus Proclaims the Good News of the Kingdom of God
- The Transfiguration of Jesus
- The Institution of the Eucharist

Sign of the Cross
(see *Catechism,* number 232)
In the name of the Father, and of the Son, and of the Holy Spirit. Amen.

Stations of the Cross
1. Jesus is condemned to death.
2. Jesus takes up his cross.
3. Jesus falls the first time.
4. Jesus meets his mother.
5. Simon helps Jesus carry the cross.
6. Veronica wipes the face of Jesus.
7. Jesus falls the second time.
8. Jesus meets the women of Jerusalem.
9. Jesus falls the third time.
10. Jesus is stripped of his garments.
11. Jesus is nailed to the cross.
12. Jesus dies on the cross.
13. Jesus is taken down from the cross.
14. Jesus is laid in the tomb.

Catholic Terms and Definitions

abortion. The deliberate termination of a pregnancy by killing the unborn child. The Roman Catholic Church considers such direct abortion a grave contradiction of the moral law and a crime against human life.

absolution. An essential part of the sacrament of Penance and Reconciliation in which the priest pardons the sins of the person confessing, in the name of God and the Church.

abstinence. The avoidance of a particular kind of food as an act of penance or spiritual discipline; in Catholicism, the avoidance of meat on certain days.

Act of Contrition. A prayer of sorrow for one's sins, a promise to make things right, and a commitment to avoid those things that lead to sin. Such a prayer can be said anytime, but is always part of the sacrament of Penance and Reconciliation.

adoration. The prayerful acknowledgment that God is God and Creator of all that is.

adultery. Sexual activity between two persons, at least one of whom is married to another. Prohibited by the sixth commandment.

Advent. The four-week liturgical season during which Christians prepare themselves for the celebration of Christmas.

almsgiving. Freely giving money or material goods to a person who is needy. It may be an act of penance or of Christian charity.

amen. A Hebrew word meaning "let it be so" or "let it be done." As a conclusion to prayer, it represents the agreement by the person praying to what has been said in the prayer.

angel. Based on a word meaning "messenger," a personal and immortal creature, with intelligence and free will, who constantly glorifies God and serves as a messenger of God to humans in order to carry out God's saving plan.

annulment. A declaration by the Church that a marriage is null and void, that is, it never existed. Catholics who divorce must also have the marriage annulled by the Church in order to be free to marry again in the Church.

Annunciation. The biblical event in which the angel Gabriel visits the virgin Mary and announces that she is to be the mother of the Savior.

Anointing of the Sick. One of the seven sacraments, sometimes formerly known as "the sacrament of the dying," in which a gravely ill, aging, or dying person is anointed by the priest and prayed over by him and attending believers. One need not be dying to receive the sacrament.

Apostles. The general term *apostle* means "one who is sent," and can be used in reference to any missionary of the Church during the New Testament period. In reference to the twelve companions chosen by Jesus, also known as "the Twelve," the term refers to those special witnesses of Jesus on whose ministry the early Church was built, and whose successors are the bishops.

apostolic fathers. A group of Greek Christian authors in the late first and early second centuries. They are our chief source of information about the early Church, and may have historical connections to the Apostles.

apostolic succession. The uninterrupted passing on of authority from the Apostles directly to all bishops. It is accomplished through the laying on of hands when a bishop is ordained.

Apostolic Tradition. *See* Tradition.

apparition. An appearance to people on Earth of a heavenly being—Christ, Mary, an angel, or a saint. The New Testament includes stories of multiple apparitions by Jesus between Easter and his Ascension into heaven.

arms race. The competition between nations to build up stockpiles of weapons of all kinds, including weapons of mass destruction. Many of these stockpiles are large enough to destroy the world several times over.

artificial insemination. The process by which a man's sperm and a woman's egg are united in a manner other than natural sexual intercourse. In the narrowest sense, it means injecting sperm into a woman's cervical canal. The Church considers it morally wrong because it separates intercourse from the act of procreation.

Ascension. The "going up" into heaven of the risen Christ forty days after his Resurrection.

assembly. Also known as a congregation, it is a community of believers gathered for worship as the Body of Christ.

Assumption of Mary. The dogma that recognizes that the body of the Blessed Virgin Mary was taken directly to heaven after her life on Earth had ended.

atheist; atheism. One who denies the existence of God; and the denial of the existence of God.

Baptism. The first of the seven sacraments, by which one becomes a member of the Church and a new creature in Christ; the first of the three sacraments of initiation, the others being Confirmation and the Eucharist.

Baptism of blood. The Catholic Church's firm conviction that someone who dies for the faith without being baptized actually receives Baptism through his or her death.

Beatitudes. The teachings of Jesus during the Sermon on the Mount in which he describes the actions and attitudes that should characterize Christians, and by which one can discover genuine meaning and happiness.

benediction. In general, another name for a blessing prayer. For Catholics, it more often refers to the prayer in which the Blessed Sacrament is used to bless the people.

Bible. The collection of Christian sacred writings, or Scriptures, accepted by the Church as inspired by God, and composed of the Old and New Testaments.

bishop. Based on a word for "overseer," one who has received the fullness of the sacrament of Holy Orders, is a member of the "college" of bishops, and is recognized as a successor of the Apostles. When he serves as head of a diocese, he is often referred to as the ordinary or local bishop.

blasphemy. Speaking, acting, or thinking about God in a way that is irreverent, mocking, or offensive. It is a sin against the second commandment.

Blessed Sacrament. Another name for the Eucharist, especially for the consecrated bread and wine when they are reserved in the tabernacle for adoration or for distribution to the sick.

blessing. A prayer asking that God care for a particular person, place, or activity. A simple blessing is usually made with the sign of the cross.

Body of Christ. A term which when capitalized designates Jesus's body in the Eucharist, or the entire Church, which is also referred to as the Mystical Body of Christ.

breviary. A prayer book that contains the prayers for the Liturgy of the Hours.

brothers. *See* religious life, congregation, order.

calumny. Ruining the reputation of another person by lying or spreading rumors. It is also called slander, and is a sin against the seventh commandment.

canon. This word has a variety of meanings. The canon of the Scriptures refers to the Church's list of books of the Bible. The canon of the Mass is another name for the Eucharistic prayer. Canon law is the official body of laws for Catholics.

canonization. The official proclamation by the Pope that a deceased member of the Church is to be recognized as a saint and may serve as a model of the Christian ideal for all believers; also the name of the process by which one is found worthy of such recognition.

capital punishment. Another name for the death penalty, a sentence sometimes given to people who commit serious crimes. The Church teaches that the necessity for capital punishment in today's world is rare.

cardinal virtues. Based on the Latin word for "pivot," four virtues that are viewed as pivotal or essential for full Christian living: prudence, justice, fortitude, and temperance.

catechesis. Based on a word meaning "to echo," the process of education and formation of Christians of all ages, by which they are taught the essentials of Christian doctrine and are formed as disciples of Jesus. Those who serve as ministers of catechesis are called catechists.

catechism. A popular summary, usually in book form, of Catholic doctrine about faith and morals and commonly intended for use within programs of formal catechesis. The official and most authoritative Catholic catechism is the *Catechism of the Catholic Church.*

catechumen. One who is preparing for full initiation into the Catholic Church by engaging in formal study, reflection, and prayer.

catechumenate. The name of the full process, as well as of one formal stage within the process, by which persons are prepared for full initiation into the Church. The process is commonly reserved for adult converts to Catholicism.

cathedral. Based on a word for "chair," the official Church of the bishop of a diocese, at which he is recognized as the chief pastor. The bishop's "chair" symbolizes his teaching and governing authority within the diocese.

Catholic Church. The name given to the universal group of Christian communities that is in communion with the Pope, the successor of Peter. It was established by Christ on the foundation of his Apostles.

celebrant. The person who oversees any act of public worship. In a Eucharistic liturgy or Mass, the celebrant is always an ordained priest.

celibacy. The state or condition of those who have chosen or taken vows to remain unmarried in order to devote themselves entirely to service of the Church and the Kingdom of God. *See also* vow(s).

charism. A special gift or grace of the Holy Spirit given to an individual Christian or a community, commonly for the benefit and building up of the entire Church.

charity. The theological virtue by which we love God above all things and, out of that love of God, love our neighbor as ourselves.

chastity. The virtue by which people are able successfully and healthfully to integrate their sexuality into their total person; recognized as one of the fruits of the Holy Spirit. Also, one of the vows of the religious life.

chief priests. In biblical Judaism, the priests (descendants of the tribe of Levi) were responsible for the proclamation of God's will, the interpretation of the Law, and worship and ritual sacrifice in the synagogues. Jesus often found himself in conflict with them.

chrism. Perfumed oil, consecrated by the bishop, which is used for special anointings in Baptism, Confirmation, and Holy Orders. It signifies the gift of the Holy Spirit.

Christ. *See* Jesus Christ.

Christmas. The feast day on which Christians celebrate the birth of Jesus; also refers to the liturgical season that immediately follows Christmas Day.

church. In common Christian usage, the term *church* is used in three related ways: (1) the entire people of God throughout the world; (2) the diocese, which is also known as the local church; and (3) the assembly of believers gathered for celebration of the liturgy, especially the Eucharist. In the creed, the Church is recognized as one, holy, catholic, and apostolic—traits which together are referred to as "marks of the Church."

civil authorities. The people in society who are responsible for making and enforcing civil laws. They have a responsibility for safeguarding human freedom and human dignity.

civil disobedience. Deliberate refusal to obey a law prescribed by the state, usually on moral grounds.

civil laws. The laws that govern society. Civil laws should reflect the natural law that God has placed in every human heart.

clergy. In the Catholic Church, the term refers to men who receive the sacrament of Holy Orders as deacons, priests, or bishops. In the broader Church, the term refers to anyone ordained for ministry.

college of bishops. The assembly of bishops, headed by the Pope, that holds the teaching authority and responsibility in the Church.

commandments. In general, a norm or guide for moral behavior; commonly, the Ten Commandments given by God to Moses. Jesus summarized all the commandments within the twofold or Great Commandments to love God and neighbor.

common good. Social conditions that allow for all citizens of the earth, individuals and families, to meet basic needs and achieve fulfillment.

communion of saints. The spiritual union of all those who believe in Christ and have been redeemed, including both those who have died and those who are still living.

concupiscence. The tendency of all human beings toward sin, as a result of original sin.

confession, private. Telling one's sins to a priest. It is an essential element of the sacrament of Penance and Reconciliation.

confidentiality. Keeping safe a truth that must not be shared with others because to do so would be immoral or illegal.

confirmand. A candidate for the sacrament of Confirmation.

Confirmation. With Baptism and the Eucharist, one of the three sacraments of initiation. Through an outpouring of special gifts of the Holy Spirit, Confirmation completes the grace of Baptism by confirming or "sealing" the baptized person's union with Christ and by equipping that person for active participation in the life of the Church.

congregation. *See* assembly.

conscience. The "interior voice" of a person, a God-given internal sense of what is morally wrong or right. Conscience leads people to understand themselves as responsible for their actions, and prompts them to do good and avoid evil. To make good judgments, one needs to have a well-formed conscience.

conscientious objection. Refusal to join the military or take part in a war, based on moral or religious grounds. Conscientious objectors must seek official approval of their status from the government.

consecrated life. A state of life recognized by the official Church in which a person publicly professes vows of poverty, chastity, and obedience.

consecration. Making a person (candidate for ordination), place (a new church), or thing (bread and wine) holy. During the Mass, the term refers to that point in the Eucharistic prayer when the priest recites Jesus's words of institution, changing the bread and wine into the body and blood of Christ.

contemplation. A form of wordless prayer in which one is fully focused on the presence of God; sometimes defined as "resting in God," a deep sense of loving adoration of God.

contraception. The deliberate attempt to interfere with the creation of new life as a result of sexual intercourse. It is considered morally wrong by the Church, which teaches that a married couple must remain open to procreation whenever they engage in sexual intercourse.

conversion. A profound change of heart, turning away from sin and toward God.

council of the Church. An official assembly of Church leaders, often for the purpose of discernment and decision making about particular issues. When represented by and concerned with the entire Church, it is called *ecumenical*, from a word meaning "the whole wide world." Councils can also be regional or local.

covenant. In general, a solemn agreement between human beings or between God and a human being in which mutual commitments are recognized; also called a testament. In the Bible, two covenants are central: (1) the Covenant between God and the ancient people of Israel established in God's Sinai Covenant with Moses; also called the Old Testament or Old Covenant; and (2) the New Covenant established by Jesus through his sacrificial death and Resurrection; also called the New Testament. The term *testament* has come to be associated primarily with the sacred Scriptures that record the history and meaning of the two biblical covenants.

Creation. The beginning of all that exists as a result of an act of God, who made everything from nothing. The story of Creation is told in the Book of Genesis.

Creator. A title given to God to signify that God and only God is the ultimate creator of everything that is and everything that ever will be.

creed. An official profession of faith, usually prepared and presented by a council of the Church and used in the Church's liturgy. Based on the Latin *credo,* meaning "I believe," the two most familiar Catholic creeds are the Apostles' Creed and the Nicene Creed.

deacon; diaconate. The third degree or level of the sacrament of Holy Orders, after that of bishop and priest. Deacons are ordained to assist priests and bishops in a variety of ministries. Some are ordained deacons as one stage of their preparation for eventual priesthood. Others do not seek priesthood but commit to lifelong ministry to the Church. The latter are known as permanent deacons.

Decalogue. Another name for the Ten Commandments. Also called the Law or the Law of Moses.

denomination. A group of religious organizations uniting under a single legal and administrative body and subscribing to the same creed and moral code.

detraction. Revealing something about another person that is true, but is harmful to his or her reputation.

devil; demon. A fallen angel, one created naturally good but who sinned against God by refusing to accept God's Reign. The term *devil* refers to Satan, Lucifer, or the Evil One, the chief of the fallen angels; demon refers to an agent of the Evil One.

diocesan priest. A man ordained by the bishop for service to the local Church in parish ministry or another diocesan apostolate.

diocese. Also known as a "particular" or "local" Church, the regional community of believers, who commonly gather in parishes, under the leadership of a bishop. At times, a diocese is determined not on the basis of geography but on the basis of language or culture.

discernment. From a Latin word meaning "to separate or to distinguish between," it is the practice of listening for God's call in our life and distinguishing between good and bad choices.

disciple. A follower of Christ. Based on a word for pupil or student, used both to designate those who learned from and followed Jesus in New Testament times (the disciples) as well as those who commit to follow him today.

dismissal rite. The final part of the liturgy, comprising a closing prayer, a blessing, and usually a closing song.

disposition. An inner attitude and readiness to receiving God's gifts (graces), particularly through the sacraments.

doctrine. An official teaching of the Church based on the Revelation of God by and through Christ.

dogma. Those teachings that are recognized as central to Church teaching, defined by the Magisterium, and accorded the fullest weight and authority. *See also* heresy.

domestic church. Another name for the first and most fundamental community of faith: the family.

doxology. A prayer of glory and praise to one God in three divine persons. Two examples of doxologies from the Mass are the Glory to God and the words that precede the great Amen.

Easter. The day on which Christians celebrate Jesus's Resurrection from the dead; considered the most holy of all days and the climax of the Church's liturgical year. *See also* Triduum.

ecumenical council. A gathering of all Catholic bishops, convened by the Pope and under his authority and guidance. The last ecumenical council was Vatican II, called by Pope John XXIII in 1962.

ecumenism. The movement to restore unity among the Christian Churches and, ultimately, of all humans throughout "the whole wide world" (the literal meaning of the word).

efficacious. The power something holds to cause a desired effect. The sacraments are efficacious in bringing about the spiritual reality that they signify.

embezzlement. The sin of taking funds that are not yours, from a business, an organization, or the government.

encyclical. A letter written by the Pope and sent to the whole Church and, at times, beyond the Church to the whole world; commonly focused on Church teaching regarding a particular issue or currently important matter.

envy. Jealousy, resentment, or sadness because of another person's good fortune. It is one of the capital sins, and contrary to the tenth commandment.

Eucharist, the. Also called the Mass or Lord's Supper, and based on a word for "thanksgiving," the central Christian liturgical celebration; established by Jesus at the Last Supper. In the Eucharist, the sacrificial death and Resurrection of Jesus is both remembered ("Do this in memory of me") and renewed ("This is my body, given for you"). The Sunday celebration of the Eucharist is considered the heart of the Church's life and worship, and participation in it is expected of all Catholics of the age and ability to do so.

Eucharistic adoration. A type of prayer in which one meditates before the Blessed Sacrament, either privately or during a communal prayer such as benediction.

Eucharistic prayer. The part of the Mass that includes the consecration of the bread and wine. It begins with the preface and concludes with the great Amen.

euthanasia. A direct action, or a deliberate lack of action, that causes the death of a handicapped, sick, or dying person. Some attempt to justify it as an act of mercy intended to relieve suffering, but the Catholic Church rejects that position, and considers euthanasia a violation of the fifth commandment against killing.

evangelist. Based on a word for "good news," in general, anyone who actively works to spread the Gospel of Jesus; more commonly and specifically, one of the persons traditionally recognized as authors of the four Gospels: Matthew, Mark, Luke, and John.

evangelization. The proclamation of the Gospel of Jesus through word and witness.

examination of conscience; examen. Prayerful reflection on and assessment of one's own words, attitudes, and actions in light of the Gospel of Jesus; more specifically, the conscious evaluation of one's life in preparation for reception of the sacrament of Penance and Reconciliation.

exorcism. A power given to the Church, in the name of Jesus Christ, to free or protect a person or object from the power of the devil.

exposition. As part of Eucharistic adoration, exposition is the custom of taking the Eucharist from the tabernacle and placing it in a special vessel called a monstrance, designed to hold a host and "expose" it—that is, to make it visible—so that people can pray before it.

faith. In general, the belief in the existence of God. For Christians, the gift of God by which one freely accepts God's full Revelation in Jesus Christ. It is a matter of both the head (acceptance of Church teaching regarding the Revelation of God) and the heart (love of God and neighbor as a response to God's first loving us); also, one of the three theological virtues.

fall, the. Also called the fall from grace, the biblical revelation about the origins of sin and evil in the world, expressed figuratively in the story of Adam and Eve in Genesis. *See also* original sin.

fasting. Refraining from food and drink as an act of spiritual discipline or as an expression of sorrow for sin; sometimes required by the Church, especially during the liturgical season of Lent.

Father. The name for God used most commonly by Jesus and, therefore, held in high esteem by the Church. *See also* Trinity.

final judgment. The judgment of the human race by Jesus Christ at his Second Coming, as noted in the Nicene Creed. It is also called the last judgment.

first Friday. A particular devotion to the sacred heart of Jesus that involves receiving the Eucharist on nine consecutive first Fridays of the month. According to Tradition, those who do so will receive special graces.

fornication. Sexual intercourse between a man and a woman who are not married. It is morally wrong to engage in intercourse before marriage, and it is a sin against the sixth commandment.

fortitude. Also called strength or courage, the virtue that enables one to maintain sound moral judgment and behavior in the face of difficulties and challenges; one of the four cardinal virtues.

forty hours' devotion. A three-day period of worship of the Blessed Sacrament, approximately equaling the time Jesus lay in the tomb. The Blessed Sacrament is exposed in a monstrance during this time.

free will. The gift from God that allows human beings to choose from among various actions, for which we are held accountable. It is the basis for moral responsibility.

fruits of the Holy Spirit. The characteristics and qualities of those who allow themselves to be guided by the Holy Spirit. They are listed in Galatians 5:22–23.

fundamentalism. An interpretation of the Bible and Christian doctrine based on the literal meaning of the words and without regard to the historical setting in which the writings or teachings were first developed; the person who holds such a perspective is called a fundamentalist.

gathering rite. The opening of the liturgy, designed to prepare the assembly for the celebration. It consists of the opening procession, the penitential rite, the Glory to God, and an opening prayer.

genetic engineering. Manipulating the genetic code of plants, animals, or human beings to alter it in some way. Such activity with human DNA is considered a violation of the sanctity of life.

genuflection. Kneeling on one knee as a sign of reverence for the Blessed Sacrament.

gifts of the Holy Spirit. Special graces given to us by the Holy Spirit to help us respond to God's call to holiness. The list of seven gifts is derived from Isaiah 11:1–3.

God. The infinite and divine being recognized as the source and creator of all that exists. *See also* Trinity.

Gospel. Most basically, "the good news" (the phrase on which the word *gospel* is based) of the Revelation of God in and through Jesus Christ, proclaimed initially by him, then by the Apostles, and now by the Church; also refers to those four books of the New Testament that focus on the person, life, teachings, death, and Resurrection of Jesus.

grace. The free and undeserved gift of God's loving and active presence in the universe and in our life. *See also* sanctifying grace.

healing, sacraments of. The two sacraments that are concerned with healing the mind, body, and spirit: the sacrament of Anointing of the Sick and the sacrament of Penance and Reconciliation.

heaven. Traditionally, the dwelling place of God and the saints, meaning all who are saved; more accurately, not a place but a state of eternal life and union with God, in which one experiences full happiness and the satisfaction of the deepest human longings.

hell. The state of permanent separation from God, reserved for those who freely and consciously choose to reject God to the very end of their life.

heresy. The conscious and deliberate rejection of a dogma of the Church. *See also* doctrine; dogma.

hierarchy. In general, the line of authority in the Church; more narrowly, the Pope and bishops, as successors of the Apostles, in their authoritative role as leaders of the Church. *See also* Magisterium.

Holy Communion. Another name for the Eucharist, the body and blood of Jesus Christ.

holy days of obligation. Feast days in the liturgical year on which, in addition to Sundays, Catholics are obliged to participate in the Eucharist.

Holy Orders. The sacrament by which members of the Church are ordained for permanent ministry in the Church as bishops, priests, or deacons.

Holy Spirit. The third person of the Blessed Trinity, understood as the perfect love between God the Father and the Son, Jesus Christ, who inspires, guides, and sanctifies the life of believers. *See also* Trinity.

holy water. Blessed water used in ritual sprinklings or when making the sign of the cross as a reminder of Baptism.

Holy Week. In the Church's liturgical year, the week preceding Easter, beginning with Palm Sunday; it culminates the annual celebration of Christ's Passion, death, and Resurrection.

homosexuality. A sexual attraction to members of one's own gender. The Church teaches that homosexual activity is morally wrong.

hope. The theological virtue by which we trust in the promises of God and expect from God both eternal life and the grace we need to attain it; the conviction that God's grace is at work in the world and that the Kingdom of God established by and through Jesus Christ is becoming realized through the workings of the Holy Spirit among us.

human dignity. The idea that because all people are created in God's image, they have fundamental worth. This notion is the foundation of Catholic social teaching.

human rights. The basic political, social, and economic rights that every human being claims, by virtue of their human dignity as beings created by God. Society cannot grant these rights and must not violate them.

humility. The virtue by which one understands that one is totally dependent on God, and also appreciates and uses properly the gifts she or he has been given by God.

idolatry. Worship of other beings, creatures, or material goods in a way that is fitting for God alone. It is a violation of the first commandment.

Ignatian Gospel contemplation. A prayer form that uses the imagination to immerse a person in a story from the Scriptures, in order to better understand the story's meaning.

Immaculate Conception. The Catholic dogma that the Blessed Virgin Mary was free from sin from the first moment of her conception.

immortality. The quality or state of unending, everlasting life; the Catholic doctrine that the human soul survives the death of the body and remains in existence, to be reunited with the body at the final resurrection; identified in the creed as belief in "the resurrection of the body and life everlasting."

Incarnation. Based on words meaning "in flesh," the mystery and Church dogma that the Son of God assumed human nature and "became flesh" in the person of Jesus of Nazareth. The Incarnation means that Jesus, the Son of God and second person of the Trinity, is both fully God and fully man.

indissolubility. A property of the sacrament of Marriage that excludes any possibility for breaking the marital bond.

inerrancy. The fact that the books of the Scriptures are free from error regarding the spiritual and religious truth that God wishes to reveal through them for the sake of our salvation. *See also* inspiration, biblical.

infallibility; infallible. The gift of the Spirit to the whole Church by which the leaders of the Church—the Pope and the bishops in union with him—are protected from fundamental error when formulating a specific teaching on a matter of faith and morals.

initiation. The process by which a nonbaptized person is prepared to become a full member of the Church. The three sacraments of initiation are Baptism, Confirmation, and the Eucharist.

inspiration, biblical. The guidance of the Holy Spirit in the development of the Scriptures, whereby the Spirit guided the human authors to teach without error those truths of God that are necessary for our salvation. It is on the basis of inspiration that we can call the Bible the word of God.

intercession. A prayer on behalf of another person or group.

in vitro fertilization. The fertilization of a woman's ovum (egg) with a man's sperm outside of her body. The fertilized egg is transferred to the woman's uterus. The process is considered to be a moral violation of the dignity of procreation.

Islam. Founded by the prophet Muhammad, it is one of the three great religions of the Western world, with connections to both Judaism and Christianity. The holy scriptures of the faith are gathered in the Qur'an.

Israelites. The chosen People of God; members of the twelve tribes descended from Jacob who inhabited the land of Israel during biblical times.

Jesus Christ. The Son of God, the second person of the Trinity, who took on flesh in Jesus of Nazareth. *Jesus* in Hebrew means, "God saves," and was the name given the historical Jesus at the Annunciation. *Christ,* based on the word for "Messiah," meaning "the anointed one," is a title that was given Jesus by the Church after his full identity was revealed.

Judaism. The religious practices, beliefs, perspectives, and philosophies of the Jewish people. The biblical roots are in the Hebrew Scriptures, particularly in the Torah (which is also the first five books of the Bible). The Jews also have a rich wisdom tradition handed down to them from their rabbis (teachers).

justice. The cardinal virtue concerned with rights and duties within relationships; the commitment, as well as the actions and attitudes that flow from the commitment, to ensure that all persons—particularly the poor and oppressed—receive what is due them.

justification. God's act of bringing a sinful human being into right relationship with him. It involves removal of sin and the gift of God's sanctifying grace to renew holiness.

just war. War involves many evils, no matter the circumstances. For a war to be just, it must be declared by a lawful authority, and there must be just cause, the right intention (such as self-defense), and weapons must be used in a way that protects the life of innocent people.

Kingdom of God. The reign or rule of God over the hearts of people and, as a consequence of that, the development of a new social order based on unconditional love. Also called the Reign of God.

Kyrie Eleison. Greek for "Lord, have mercy." The short prayer, along with its counterpart, Christe Eleison, "Christ, have mercy," is part of the penitential rite at the beginning of a Eucharistic liturgy.

laity. All members of the Church, with the exception of those who are ordained. The laity share in Christ's role as priest, prophet, and king, witnessing to God's love and power in the world.

Last Supper. A supper during the Jewish celebration of Passover that was the last meal Jesus shared with his disciples before being handed over for crucifixion. It is remembered by Catholics as the occasion of the first Eucharist, and is commemorated by believers on Holy Thursday.

Law, the. Another name for the Ten Commandments, it is also called the Law of Moses or the Old Law.

lectio divina. A form of meditative prayer, usually focused on a passage from the Scriptures, that involves repetitive readings and periods of reflection; can serve as either private or communal prayer.

lectionary. The official liturgical book from which the readings selected for the liturgy of the word during Mass are proclaimed. The person who proclaims the word is called a lector.

legitimate defense. The teaching that limited violence is morally acceptable in defending yourself or your nation from an attack.

Lent. The liturgical season of forty days that begins with Ash Wednesday and ends with the celebration of the Paschal mystery in the Easter Triduum, the season during which believers focus on penance for sin.

liturgical celebration. *See* liturgy.

liturgical year. The annual cycle of religious feasts and seasons that forms the context for the Church's worship. (See also the section on Catholic beliefs and practices for a list of seasons.)

liturgist. One who has the training and responsibility for planning and coordinating all aspects of the worship life of a faith community.

liturgy. Based on a word meaning "public work," the official public worship of the Church, the heart and high point—or source and goal—of which is the Eucharist.

liturgy of the Eucharist. The second major part of the Mass, it comprises the preparation of gifts, the Eucharistic prayer, and the rite of Holy Communion.

Liturgy of the Hours. The official, nonsacramental daily prayer of the Catholic Church. The prayer provides standard prayers, Scripture readings, and reflections at regular hours throughout the day. *See also* breviary.

liturgy of the word. The first major part of the Mass, it comprises three scriptural readings, a responsorial psalm, a homily, the Nicene Creed, and petitions.

living wage. Also called just wage, it is a fair payment that a worker receives from an employer, which allows the wage earner and his or her family to live a life of dignity and meet basic needs.

Lord. The Old Testament name for God that in speaking or reading aloud was automatically substituted for the name Yahweh, which was considered too sacred to be spoken; in the New Testament, used for both God the Father and, on occasion, for Jesus, to reflect awareness of Jesus's identity as the Son of God.

Lord's Day. Another name for Sunday and holy days of obligation. Catholics are required to attend Mass on these days and refrain from any work that might stand in the way of relaxation and renewal of mind and body.

Lord's Prayer. Another name for the Our Father. (See also the section on Catholic prayers and devotions.)

love. The human longing for God and a selfless commitment to supporting the dignity and humanity of all people, simply because they are created in God's image. Also called "charity," it is one of the three theological virtues.

lust. Intense and uncontrolled desire for sexual pleasure. It is one of the seven capital sins.

Magisterium. The name given the official teaching authority of the Church, whose task is to interpret and preserve the truths of the Church revealed in both the Scriptures and Tradition.

Magnificat. Mary's prayer of praise when she visited her cousin Elizabeth. It is recorded in Luke 1:46–55. The name of the prayer is the first word of the prayer in Latin, which means "magnify."

marks of the Church. The four characteristics of the true Church of Jesus Christ: one, holy, catholic (universal), and apostolic. These marks are recited at Mass as part of the Nicene Creed.

marriage; Matrimony. Marriage is an exclusive, permanent, and lifelong contract between a man and a woman in which they commit to care for each other and to procreate and raise children; when the marriage takes place between baptized persons who enter into a covenant modeled on that between Christ and the Church, it is recognized as the sacrament of Matrimony. The two terms are often interchanged.

martyr. A person who voluntarily suffers death because of her or his beliefs. The Church has canonized many martyrs as saints.

Mary. The mother of Jesus, sometimes called the Blessed Virgin Mary. Because Jesus is the Son of God and the second person of the Trinity, Mary is also given the title Mother of God.

Mass. Another name for the Eucharist. Based on the Latin word *missa,* meaning "to be sent," it refers to the dismissal, in which worshipers are told to "go in peace to love and serve the Lord."

masturbation. Self-manipulation of one's sexual organs for the purpose of erotic pleasure or to achieve orgasm. The Church considers masturbation to be a sin because the act cannot result in the creation of a new life. It is also wrong because it is self-serving, and God created sex not for self-gratification but to unify a husband and wife in marriage.

meditation. A form of prayer involving a variety of methods and techniques, in which one engages the mind, imagination, and emotions in order to focus on a particular truth, biblical theme, or other spiritual matter.

ministry. Based on a word for service, in a general sense any service offered to help the Church fulfill its mission; more narrowly, particular expressions of such service (for example, the ministry of catechesis and liturgical ministries).

miracle. A special manifestation, or sign, of the presence and power of God active in human history.

modesty. From the same root word as "moderation," it means keeping one's attitudes, actions, speech, dress, and other behaviors controlled in a way that acknowledges one's own dignity.

monotheism. Belief in one God instead of many.

monstrance. The special vessel designed to hold a host and make it visible for Eucharistic adoration.

morality. Dealing with the goodness or evil of human acts, attitudes, and values; involves matters such as right judgment, decision-making skills, personal freedom and responsibility, and so on.

mortal sin. An action so contrary to the will of God that it results in a complete separation from God and God's grace. As a consequence of that separation, the person is condemned to eternal death. To be a mortal sin requires three conditions: it must involve grave matter, the person must have full knowledge of the evil of the act, and the person must give his or her full consent in committing the act.

mysticism. An intense experience of the presence and power of God, resulting in a deeper sense of union with God; those who regularly experience such union are called mystics.

natural law. Our God-given instinct to be in right relationship with God, other people, the world, and ourselves. The basis for natural law is our participation in God's wisdom and goodness because we are created in the divine likeness. The fundamental expressions of natural law remain fixed and unchanging, which is why natural law is the foundation for both personal morality and civil norms.

New Law. The law of the Gospel of Jesus Christ, it is a law of love, grace, and freedom. It is distinguished from the Old Law, or the Law of Moses.

New Testament. The twenty-seven books of the Bible written during the early years of the Church in response to the life, mission, death, and Resurrection of Jesus; also, another name for the New Covenant established between God and humanity by Jesus.

Nicene Creed. The formal statement or profession of faith commonly recited during the Eucharist. *See also* creed.

novena. From the Latin word for "nine," it is a public or private devotion that extends for a period of nine days. In some cases a novena is offered on a designated day for nine weeks or nine months.

nuns. *See* religious life, congregation, order.

obedience. Based on a word meaning to hear or listen, the willingness and commitment to submit to the will of God, as well as to Church teachings and practices that reflect the will of God. *See also* vow(s).

oil of the sick. The oil used in the sacrament of the Anointing of the Sick. It is blessed by the bishop along with other holy oils during the annual chrism Mass.

Old Law. The Law of Moses, the Ten Commandments. It contrasts to the New Law of the Gospel.

Old Testament. The forty-six books of the Bible that record the history of salvation from Creation, through the story of ancient Israel, and up to the time of Jesus; also refers to the Old Covenant established between God and the people of Israel in God's encounter with Moses on Mount Sinai.

ordained ministers. Those who have received the sacrament of Holy Orders, that is, deacons, priests, and bishops.

Ordinary Time. The time in the liturgical year that is not part of a special season like Advent, Christmas, Lent, or Easter.

ordination. *See* Holy Orders.

original sin. The sin by which the first humans disobeyed God, resulting in separation from God; also, the state of human nature that affects every person now born into the world. *See also* fall, the.

papacy. The name given the office and authority of the Bishop of Rome, the Pope. As the successor of Saint Peter, the Pope serves as both a symbol and an agent of the unity of all believers.

parable. A story intended to convey a religious truth or particular teaching through the use of metaphors; a central feature of Jesus's teaching ministry.

Paraclete. A name for the Holy Spirit, based on a word for helper or advocate.

parish. A specific community of believers, commonly but not always defined geographically, whose pastoral and spiritual care is guided by a priest or other leader appointed by a bishop.

Parousia, Christ's. The Second Coming of Christ, when his Kingdom will be fully established and his triumph over evil will be complete.

Paschal lamb. A name for Jesus, whose death and Resurrection redeemed humanity. The name is associated with Passover, a commemoration of the deliverance of the Jewish people from Egypt. To avoid the slaughter of firstborn sons by the Egyptian army, the Jews sprinkled the blood of a lamb on their doorposts.

Paschal mystery. The term given the entire process of God's plan of salvation by which God redeemed humanity from sin in and through Jesus's life, death, Resurrection, and Ascension into glory. Christians enter into the Paschal mystery through sacramental initiation, and participate in it by faithfully living out the process of dying and rising that characterizes all life.

Passion, the. The suffering and death of Jesus.

pastoral. Refers to the daily life of the Church, especially as it takes place at parish and diocesan levels. Based on a word for shepherd or shepherding, the person who tends to the pastoral care of a community is commonly called the pastor.

penance. In general, an attitude of the heart in which one experiences regret for past sin and commits to a change in behavior or attitudes; particular acts of penance may include the practice of spiritual disciplines such as prayer or fasting, or participation in the sacrament of Penance and Reconciliation.

penance, communal. The sacrament of Penance and Reconciliation celebrated within a gathering of a faith community. The most common form includes opportunities for individual confession and absolution.

Penance and Reconciliation, sacrament of. One of the seven sacraments of the Church, the liturgical celebration of God's forgiveness of sin, through which the sinner is reconciled with both God and the Church.

Pentecost. The biblical event following the Resurrection and Ascension of Jesus at which the Holy Spirit was poured out on his disciples; the first Pentecost is often identified as the birth of the Church. In the Christian liturgical year, the feast fifty days after Easter on which the biblical event of Pentecost is recalled and celebrated.

People of God. The biblical image for the Church. Those who share in Christ's mission as priest, prophet, and king.

perjury. The sin of lying while under an oath to tell the truth.

permanent deacon. *See* deacon, diaconate.

petition. A prayer form in which one asks God for help and forgiveness.

Pharisees. A Jewish sect during the time of Jesus known for their strict adherence to the Law and their concern with superficial matters.

plagiarism. Using another person's thoughts, creative ideas, writings, music, and so forth without permission, and presenting them as one's own. It is a form of stealing, and a sin against the seventh commandment.

polygamy. Having more than one spouse. It is contrary to the sanctity of marriage.

Pope. Based on a word for "father," the successor of Saint Peter and Bishop of Rome, who holds the office of the papacy. Often called the Holy Father.

pornography. A written description or visual portrayal of a person or action that is created or viewed with the intention of stimulating sexual feelings.

poverty. As a social reality, indeed, a social sin, a condition of material need experienced by the poor. The Church, in imitation of Jesus, expresses its central concern for the poor through its commitment to justice. As an attitude and value, a spirit of detachment from material things and a commitment to share all that one has with those who have not.

praise. A prayer of acknowledgment that God is God, giving God glory not for what he does, but simply because he is.

prayer. The lifting of mind and heart to God in praise, petition, thanksgiving, and intercession; communication with God in a relationship of love.

precepts of the Church. Sometimes called the commandments of the Church, these are obligations for all Catholics that are dictated by the laws of the Church.

preferential option. A moral obligation for individuals and for the Church that requires special attention to those who are poor, considering their needs first and above all others.

presbyter. A term used for officials in the early Church. Today it is an alternative word for priest.

priest; priesthood. The second of three degrees or "orders" in the sacrament of Holy Orders, along with bishop and deacon. The priest is called to serve the community of faith and its members by representing and assisting the bishop in teaching, governing, and presiding over the community's worship. Priests generally minister within a parish, school, or other setting within a diocese.

priesthood of the faithful. The belief that the Body of Christ is made up of priestly people who share in Christ's royal priesthood.

prostration. A prayer posture in which a person lies stretched out on the ground, face down, as a sign of adoration, submission, and humility. This posture is part of the rite of ordination.

prudence. The virtue by which a person is inclined toward choosing the moral good and avoiding evil; sometimes called the rudder virtue, because it helps steer the person through complex moral situations; related to conscience, and one of the four cardinal virtues.

purgatory. A state of final purification or cleansing which one may need to enter following death and before entry into heaven.

reason. The natural ability human beings have to know and understand truth.

Reconciliation. *See* Penance and Reconciliation, sacrament of.

redemption; Redeemer. The process by which we are "bought back" (the meaning of redeem) from slavery to sin into a right relationship with God. We are redeemed by the grace of God and through the life, death, and Resurrection of Jesus Christ. As the agent of redemption, Jesus is called the Redeemer.

Reign of God. *See* Kingdom of God.

religion. The beliefs and practices followed by those committed to the Gospel of Jesus and full participation in the life of the Church. By virtue of the first commandment, the first duty of a religious person is to worship and serve God alone.

religious life; congregation; order. A permanent state of life and an organized group of Christians, recognized by the Church, who have taken vows to live in community and to observe the disciplines of poverty, chastity, and obedience. Religious men are often called brothers, monks, or friars; religious women, sisters or nuns.

religious priests. Priests who are ordained within a religious community for service to the community and its ministries. With the permission of the local bishop, they may also lead parishes within a diocese.

religious vows. The vows, or promises, made by a person who becomes a full member of a religious community. Traditionally there are three vows: poverty, chastity, and obedience.

reparation. Making amends for something one did wrong that caused harm to another person or led to loss.

repentance. An attitude of sorrow for a sin committed and a resolution not to sin again. It is a response to God's gracious love and forgiveness.

restitution. Making things right with another person or people who have been harmed by an injustice, or returning or replacing what rightfully belongs to another.

Resurrection, the. The passage of Jesus from death to life "on the third day" after his Crucifixion; the heart of the Paschal mystery, and the basis of our hope in the resurrection of the dead.

resurrection of the dead. The Christian dogma that all those deemed righteous by God will be raised and will live forever with God in heaven; the conviction that not only our souls but also our transformed bodies will live on after death ("I believe in the resurrection of the body").

Revelation. God's self-communication and disclosure of the divine plan to humankind through Creation, events, persons, and, most fully, in Jesus Christ.

ritual. The established form of the words and actions for a ceremony that is repeated often. The actions often have a symbolic meaning, such as the anointing with chrism at Confirmation.

rosary. A popular devotion to Mary, the Mother of God.

Sabbath. In the Old Testament, the "seventh day" on which God rested after the work of Creation was completed; in Jewish Law, the weekly day of rest to remember God's work through private prayer, communal worship, and spiritual disciplines such as fasting; for Catholics, Sunday, the day on which Jesus was raised, which we are to observe with participation in the Eucharist in fulfillment of the commandment to "keep holy the Sabbath."

sacrament. In Catholic life and worship, the seven efficacious signs of God's grace, instituted by Christ and entrusted to the Church, by which divine life is dispensed to us.

sacramental character. A permanent and indelible spiritual mark on a person's soul, sealed by the Holy Spirit as a result of Baptism, Confirmation, and Holy Orders. For this reason these sacraments cannot be repeated.

sacramentals. Sacred signs (such as holy water and a crucifix) that bear some resemblance to the sacraments, but which do not carry the guarantee of God's grace associated with the seven sacraments.

sacraments at the service of communion. The name given to the two sacraments that are directed toward building up the People of God, namely Holy Orders and Marriage.

sacraments of healing. *See* healing, sacraments of.

sacraments of initiation. *See* initiation.

sacrilege. An offense against God. It is the abuse of a person, place, or thing dedicated to God and the worship of God.

saint. Someone who has been transformed by the grace of Christ and who resides in full union with God in heaven. *See also* canonization; communion of saints.

salvation. Liberation from sin and eternal union with God in heaven. Salvation is accomplished by God alone through the Paschal mystery—the dying and rising of Jesus Christ.

salvation history. The pattern of events in human history that exemplify God's presence and saving actions. In Catholic thought, all of history is salvation history, even though God's presence may not be recognized.

sanctifying grace. A supernatural gift of God by which our sins are forgiven and we are made holy. It restores our friendship with God.

scandal. An action or attitude—or the failure to act—that leads another person into sin.

scribes. In Jewish history, these were government officials and scholars of the Law of Moses. They enforced the requirements of the Law.

Scripture(s). Generally, the term for any sacred writing. For Christians, the Old and New Testaments that make up the Bible and are recognized as the word of God.

simony. Buying or selling of something spiritual, such as a grace, a sacrament, or a relic. It violates the honor of God.

sin. Any deliberate offense, in thought, word, or deed, against the will of God.

sisters. *See* religious life, congregation, order.

slander. Injuring another person's reputation by telling lies and spreading rumors. It is also called calumny.

social doctrine. The body of teaching by the Church on economic and social matters that includes moral judgments and demands for action in favor of those being harmed.

social encyclical. A letter from the Pope addressed to members of the universal Church regarding topics related to social justice, human rights, and peace.

social justice. The Church's commitment, and mandate to its members, to engage in conscious efforts to fight against, if not overcome, social sin.

social sin. The collective effect of sin over time, which corrupts society and its institutions by creating "structures of sin." Examples of social sin are racism, sexism, and institutionalized poverty.

society. A broad part of the human community that is distinguished by common values, traditions, standards of living, or conduct.

solidarity. Union of one's heart and mind with those who are poor or powerless, or who face an injustice. It is an act of Christian charity.

Son of God. Title frequently applied to Jesus Christ, which recognizes him as the second person of the Blessed Trinity.

soul. The spiritual life principle of human beings that survives after death.

spirituality. In general, the values, actions, attitudes, and behaviors that characterize a person's relationship with God and others. For Christians, a life guided by the Holy Spirit, lived out within the community of believers, and characterized by faith, hope, love, and service.

stewardship. An attitude that we do not own the gifts God has given us, but are trustees of those gifts. We have an obligation to share our time, talent, and material treasures with others.

suicide. Deliberately taking one's own life. It is a serious violation of God's Law and plan. It is usually accomplished as a result of serious mental and emotional anguish, and in such cases is not considered a free and deliberate act.

superstition. Attributing to someone or something else a power that belongs to God alone, and relying on such powers rather than trusting in God. It is a sin against the first commandment.

symbol. An object or action that points us to another reality. It leads us to look beyond our senses to consider the deeper mystery.

tabernacle. The receptacle in a church in which the consecrated bread and wine of the Eucharist is reserved for Communion for the sick and dying; sometimes the focus of private and communal prayer and adoration.

temperance. The cardinal virtue by which one moderates her or his appetites and passions in order to achieve balance in the use of created goods.

temptations. Invitations or enticements to commit an unwise or immoral act that often include a promise of a reward, to make the immoral act seem more appealing.

thanksgiving. A prayer of gratitude for the gift of life and the gifts of life.

theological virtues. The name for the God-given virtues of faith, hope, and love. These virtues enable us to know God as God and lead us to union with God in mind and heart.

theology. Literally, the study of God; the academic discipline and effort to understand, interpret, and order our experience of God and Christian faith; classically defined as "faith seeking understanding."

Theotokos. Greek for "God-bearer." It is the name given to Mary after an ecumenical council in the fifth century to affirm that she is the mother of the human Jesus and the mother of God.

Tradition. Based on a word meaning "to hand on," the central content of Catholic faith contained in both the Scriptures and in Church doctrines and dogmas, as well as the process by which that content is faithfully passed on from generation to generation, under the guidance of the Holy Spirit.

transubstantiation. In the sacrament of the Eucharist, this is the name given to the action of changing the bread and wine into the body and blood of Jesus Christ.

Triduum. The three days of the liturgical year that begins with the Mass of the Lord's Supper on Holy Thursday and ends with evening prayer on Easter Sunday.

Trinity. Often referred to as the Blessed Trinity, the central Christian mystery and dogma that there is one God in three persons: Father, Son, and Holy Spirit.

venerate. An action that shows deep reverence for something sacred. For example, on Good Friday, individuals in the assembly venerate the cross by bowing before or kissing the cross.

venial sin. A less serious offense against the will of God that diminishes one's personal character and weakens but does not rupture one's relationship with God. *See also* mortal sin.

vice. A practice or a habit that leads a person to sin.

vigil for the deceased. Another name for a wake service. It is a prayer service the takes place before a funeral, to pray for the repose of the soul of the deceased and for strength for those who grieve the loss.

virginal conception and birth. The dogma that Jesus was conceived in the womb of Mary and born by the power of the Holy Spirit and without the cooperation of a human father. (Note: This is not to be confused with the Immaculate Conception of Mary.)

virtue. A good habit, one that creates within us a kind of inner readiness or attraction to move toward or accomplish moral good. The theological virtues are faith, hope, and love.

vocal prayer. A prayer that is spoken aloud or silently, such as the Lord's Prayer. It is one of the three expressions of prayer, the other two being meditation and contemplation.

vocation. A call from God to all members of the Church to embrace a life of holiness. Specifically, it refers to a call to live the holy life as an ordained minister, as a vowed religious (sister or brother), in a Christian marriage, or in single life.

vow(s). A free and conscious commitment made to other persons (as in marriage), to the Church, or to God. Religious vows—those taken by members of religious congregations or orders—commonly include poverty, chastity, and obedience.

wake service. *See* vigil for the deceased.

way of the cross. A religious devotion or exercise modeled on Jesus's Passion—his trial, walk toward his death on the cross, and burial in the tomb. Sometimes called the stations of the cross, the devotion involves meditation on each step in Jesus's journey.

worship. Adoration of God, usually expressed publicly in the Church's official liturgy as well as through other prayers and devotions.

Yahweh. The Old Testament name for God, frequently translated as "I am who I am."

Notes

10 "You have made us for . . ." Ronald Rolheiser, *The Holy Longing: The Search for a Christian Spirituality* (New York: Doubleday, 1999), page 5.

21 "Trust the past to . . ." In Mark Link, *Mission 2000: Praying Scripture in a Contemporary Way, B Cycle* (Allen, TX: Tabor Publishing, 1993), page 293.

22 "I am a little pencil . . ." In Mark Link, *Vision 2000: Praying Scripture in a Contemporary Way, A Cycle* (Allen, TX: Tabor Publishing, 1992), page 262.

36 "When we read . . ." Louis Evely, *That Man Is You* (Westminster, MD: Newman Press, 1966), page 43.

36 "Most people are . . ." In Mark Link, *Mission 2000: Praying Scripture in a Contemporary Way, B Cycle* (Allen, TX: Tabor Publishing, 1993), page 27.

39 "Christ became what we are . . ." As paraphrased by Patrick Henry, *The Ironic Christian's Companion: Finding the Marks of God's Grace in the World* (New York: Riverhead Books, 1999), page 76.

47 Donald Senior, *Jesus: A Gospel Portrait,* new and revised edition (New York: Paulist Press, 1992), page 116.

57 Mary Ellen Ashcroft and Holly Bridges, *The Journey Beckons: Reflections on the Way of the Cross* (Minneapolis: Augsburg, 2000), page xi.

76 "Christ has no body . . ." In Thomas Zanzig, *Jesus the Christ: A New Testament Portrait* (Winona, MN: Saint Mary's Press, 2000), page 245.

84 "Work as if everything . . ." In Mark Link, *Vision 2000: Praying Scripture in a Contemporary Way, A Cycle* (Allen, TX: Tabor Publishing, 1994), page 167.

86 "What does love look . . ." In Mark Link, *Vision 2000: Praying Scripture in a Contemporary Way, A Cycle* (Allen, TX: Tabor Publishing, 1992), page 19.

121 From a message by Pope John Paul II, "Youth: Builders of the Twenty-first Century," December 8, 1984. Quoted in *Origins* 14 (January 10, 1985), page 491.

123 Pope John Paul II, "Letter to Families" (given in Rome at Saint Peter's on February 2, 1994), as quoted at *www.vatican.va*, August 3, 2000.

Acknowledgments

The scriptural quotations contained herein are from the New Revised Standard Version of the Bible, Catholic Edition. Copyright © 1993 and 1989 by the Division of Christian Education of the National Council of the Churches of Christ in the United States of America. All rights reserved.

The excerpts in this book marked *Catechism of the Catholic Church* or *Catechism* are quoted, adapted, or paraphrased from the English translation of the *Catechism of the Catholic Church* for use in the United States of America. Copyright © 1994 by the United States Catholic Conference, Inc.—Libreria Editrice Vaticana. Used with permission.

The excerpts from the English translation of *Rite of Baptism for Children* © 1969, International Committee on English in the Liturgy (ICEL); from the English translation of *Rite of Confirmation, Rite of the Blessing of the Oils, Rite of Consecrating the Chrism* © 1972, ICEL; from the English translation of *The Liturgy of the Hours* © 1974, ICEL; from the English translation of *Rite of Penance* © 1974, ICEL; from the English translation of *Rite of Confirmation,* second edition © 1975, ICEL; from A *Book of Prayers* © 1982, ICEL; and from the English translation of *Rite of Christian Initiation of Adults* © 1985, ICEL, are adapted or taken from *The Rites of the Catholic Church,* volume 1, prepared by the ICEL (Collegeville, MN: Pueblo Publishing, 1990), pages 546, 514, 384, 490, 55–56, 329, 489, 711–712, 484, 500, and 490, respectively. Copyright © 1976, 1983, 1988, 1990 by Pueblo Publishing Company. Copyright © 1990 by the Order of St. Benedict. Used with permission.

The list in *"Letting Your Light Shine"* on page 15 is based on "Strategy Number 11: Proud Whip" in *Values Clarification: A Handbook of Practical Strategies for Teachers and Students,* by Sidney Simon, Leland Howe, and Howard Kirschenbaum (New York: Hart Publishing Company, Inc., 1972), pages 136–138. Copyright © 1972 by Hart Publishing Company.

The Eucharistic Prayer II on page 79 and the Easter Vigil prayer on page 106 are from the *Sacramentary,* English translation prepared by the ICEL (New York: Catholic Book Publishing Company, 1974), pages 549 and 550, and 203. Copyright © 1974 by Catholic Book Publishing Company. Used with permission.

The TRAP guide to prayer on pages 83–84 is adapted from *Catechetical Sessions on Christian Prayer,* by Laurie Delgatto and Mary Shrader (Winona, MN: Saint Mary's Press, 2004), page 64. Copyright © 2004 by Saint Mary's Press. All rights reserved.

The antiphon Grail Psalm 1 on page 89 is taken from *Christian Prayer: The Liturgy of the Hours,* English translation prepared by the ICEL (New York: Catholic Book Publishing Company, 1975), page 683. Copyright © 1975 by Catholic Book Publishing Company. Copyright © 1963 by Ladies of the Grail, administered by GIA Publications. All rights reserved. Used with permission.

The words by Mother Teresa on page 90 are from *Words to Love By . . . ,* by Mother Teresa (Notre Dame, IN: Ave Maria Press, 1983), page 79. Copyright © 1983 by Ave Maria Press.

The excerpts on the major themes of social teaching on pages 93 and 95 are from *Sharing Catholic Social Teaching: Challenges and Directions,* by the United States Conference of Catholic Bishops (USCCB) (Washington, DC: USCCB, 1998), pages 4–6. Copyright © 1998 by the United States Catholic Conference, Inc.

The quotation by Pope Paul VI on page 109 is from "Constitution on the Sacred Liturgy," *Sacrosanctum Concilium,* Solemnly Promulgated by His Holiness, number 7, at *www.vatican.va/archive/ hist_councils/ii _vatican_council/documents/vat-ii_const_19631204 _sacrosanctum-concilium_en. html,* accessed September 22, 2005.

The quotation on page 113 is from *The Works of Saint Cyril of Jerusalem,* volume 2, translated by Leo McCauley (Washington, DC: The Catholic University of America Press, 1970), page 170. Copyright © 1970 by The Catholic University of America Press.

The English translation of the "Laying On of Hands" prayer on pages 114 and 119 is from the "Rite of Confirmation" second edition. Copyright © 1975 by the International Committee on English in the Liturgy. All rights reserved. Used with permission.

"The Universal Prayer" on page 123 is adapted from the prayer by Pope Clement XI at "Prayers for All Christians," *www.rc.net/wcc/univpray.htm,* accessed September 22, 2005.

Portions of the "Catholic Beliefs and Practices" and "Catholic Prayers and Devotions" in the "Catholic Quick Facts" section are taken directly or adapted from the *Handbook for Today's Catholic,* a Redemptorist Pastoral publication (Liguori, MO: Liguori Publications, 1994). Copyright © 1994 by Liguori Publications. Used with permission.

The poem on the back cover is adapted from *The Rites of the Catholic Church,* volume 1, study edition, from the English translation of the "Rite of Confirmation," second edition, copyright © 1975 by the ICEL, prepared by the ICEL, a joint commission of Catholic Bishops' Conferences (New York: Pueblo Publishing, 1990). Copyright © 1976, 1983, 1988, 1990 by Pueblo Publishing. Used with permission.

To view copyright terms and conditions for Internet materials cited here, log on to the home pages for the referenced Web sites.

During this book's preparation, all citations, facts, figures, names, addresses, telephone numbers, Internet URL's and other information cited within were verified for accuracy. The authors and Saint Mary's press staff have made every attempt to reference current and valid sources, but we cannot guarantee the content of any source, and we are not responsible for any changes that may have occurred since our verification. If you find an error in or have a question or concern about any of the information or sources listed within, please contact Saint Mary's Press.

Photo Credits

James Shaffer: pages 15, 17, 40, and 104

Gene Plaisted/The Croisers: pages 44, 58, and 76

Wittman Photography: pages 11, 26, 37, 66, 69, 99, and 110

Endnotes Cited in Quotations from the *Catechism of the Catholic Church*

1. Cf. *1 John* 2:20,27.

2. Cf. *John* 16:13.

3. Cf. *John* 20:30.

4. *John* 20:31.

5. Cf. *Mark* 4:33–34.

6. Cf. *Matthew* 13:44–45; 22:1–14.

7. Cf. *Matthew* 21:28–32.

8. Cf. *Mark* 5:25–34; 10:52; etc.

9. *Hebrews* 9:26.

10. Saint Thomas Aquinas, *Collationes in decem praeceptis* I.

11. Cf. *John* 12:49.

12. John Paul II, *Reconciliatio et paenitentia* 16.

13. Cf. *Mark* 16:16.

14. Cf. *Roman Ritual,* Rite of Confirmation *(Ordo confirmationis),* Introduction 1.

15. St. Ambrose, De myst. 7, 42: J. P. Migne, ed., Patrologia Latina (Paris: 1841–1855) 16, 402–403.